Points in Space

vector

noun

1 Mathematics & Physics a quantity having direction as well as magnitude, esp. as determining the position of one point in space relative to another.

The drawings on these pages were hand drawn, entirely from scratch, on a computer, using Adobe Illustrator software. They contain no photographic elements. Rather, they are vector graphics; all their elements–forms, lines, and colors– are defined only by the mathematical relationships of points in space. Unlike digital photographs, which are bitmapped images composed of pixels, these drawings can be reproduced from their original files in any size, without becoming pixelated or losing their sharpness, detail, and integrity. And unlike reproductions of traditional works of art–paintings, drawings, pastels, lithographs, monoprints, etc.–every printing of an original digital work is itself an original, for it otherwise exists only as a series of ones and zeros in a tiny chip of silicon.

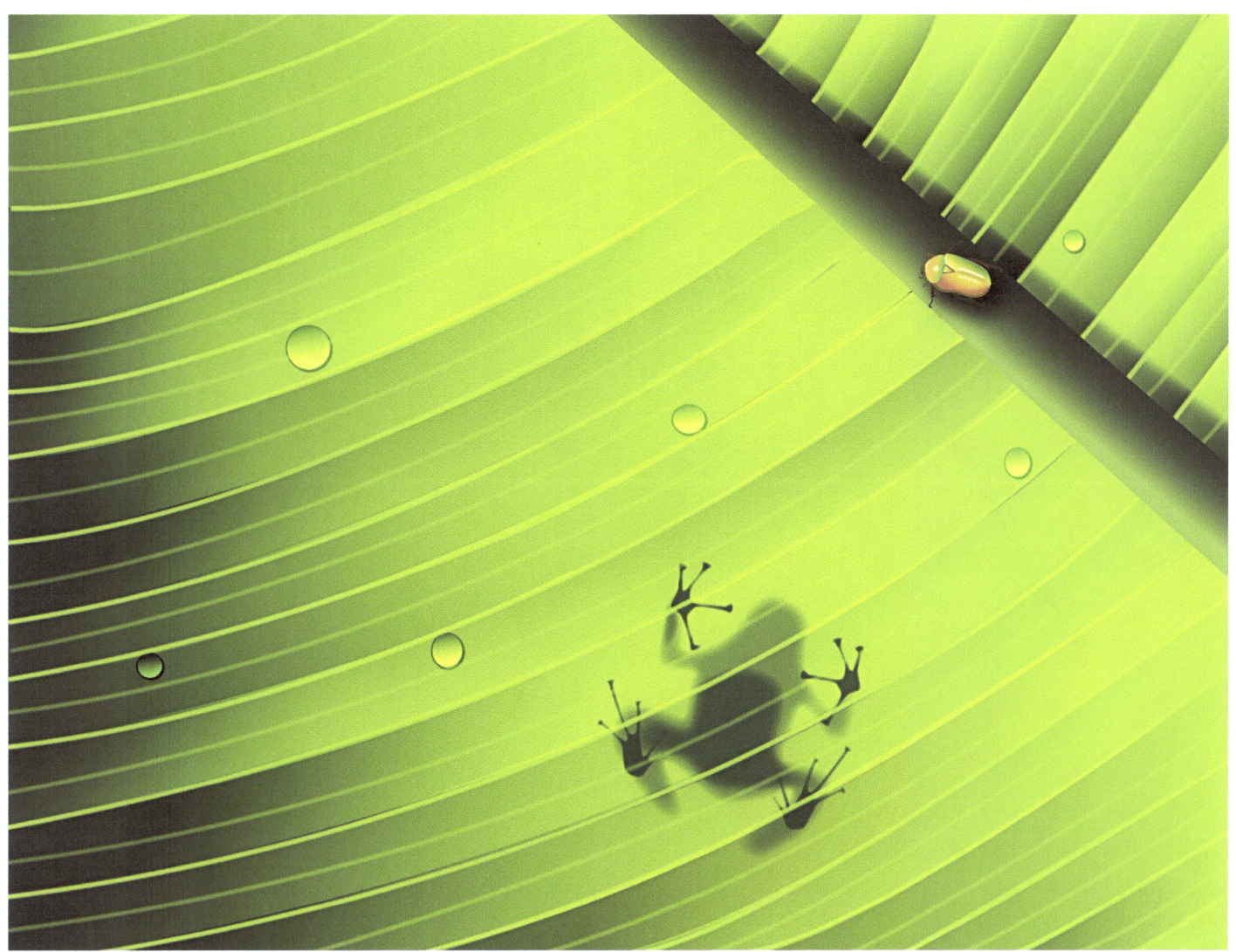

Parallel Universes

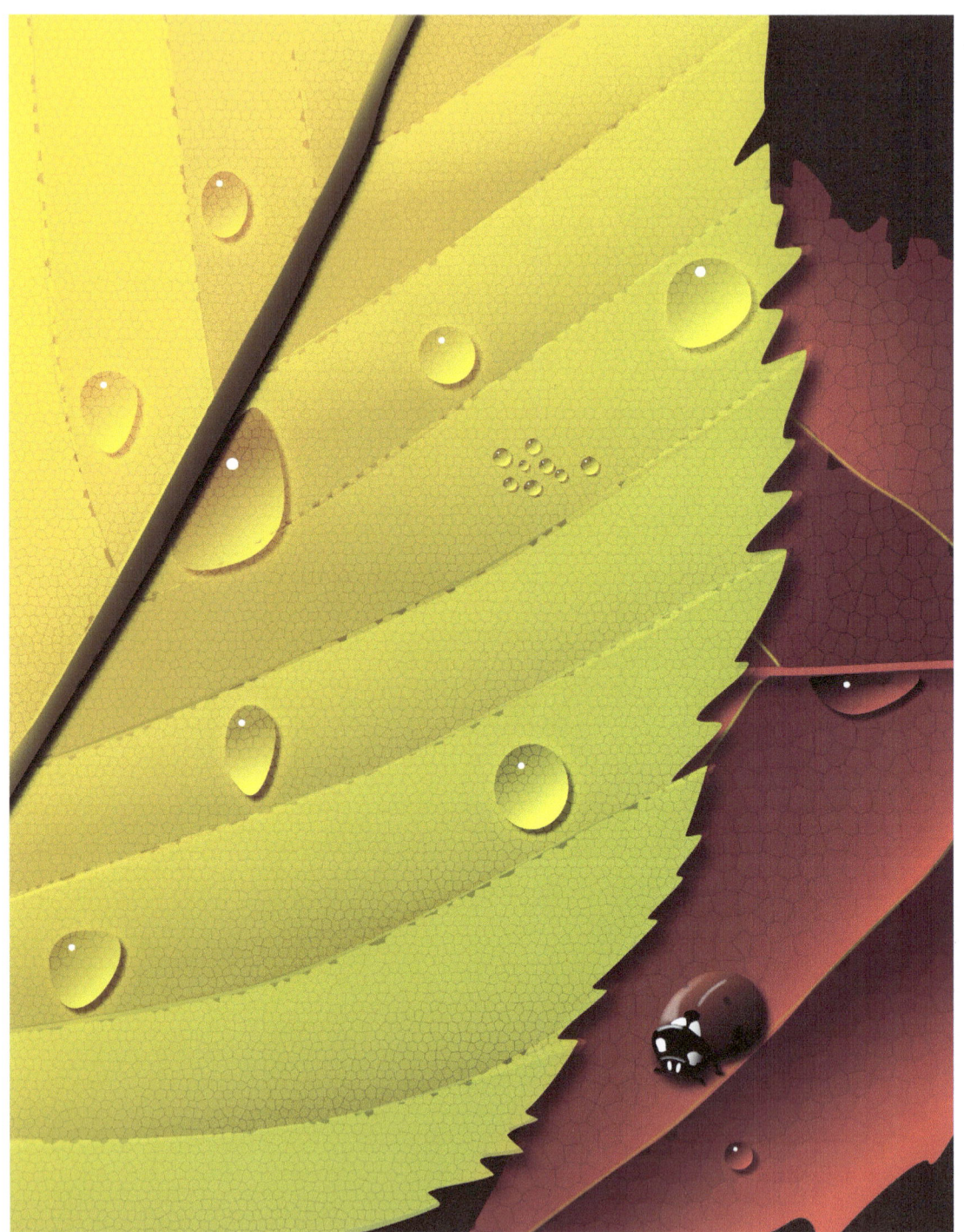

Birch Leaf

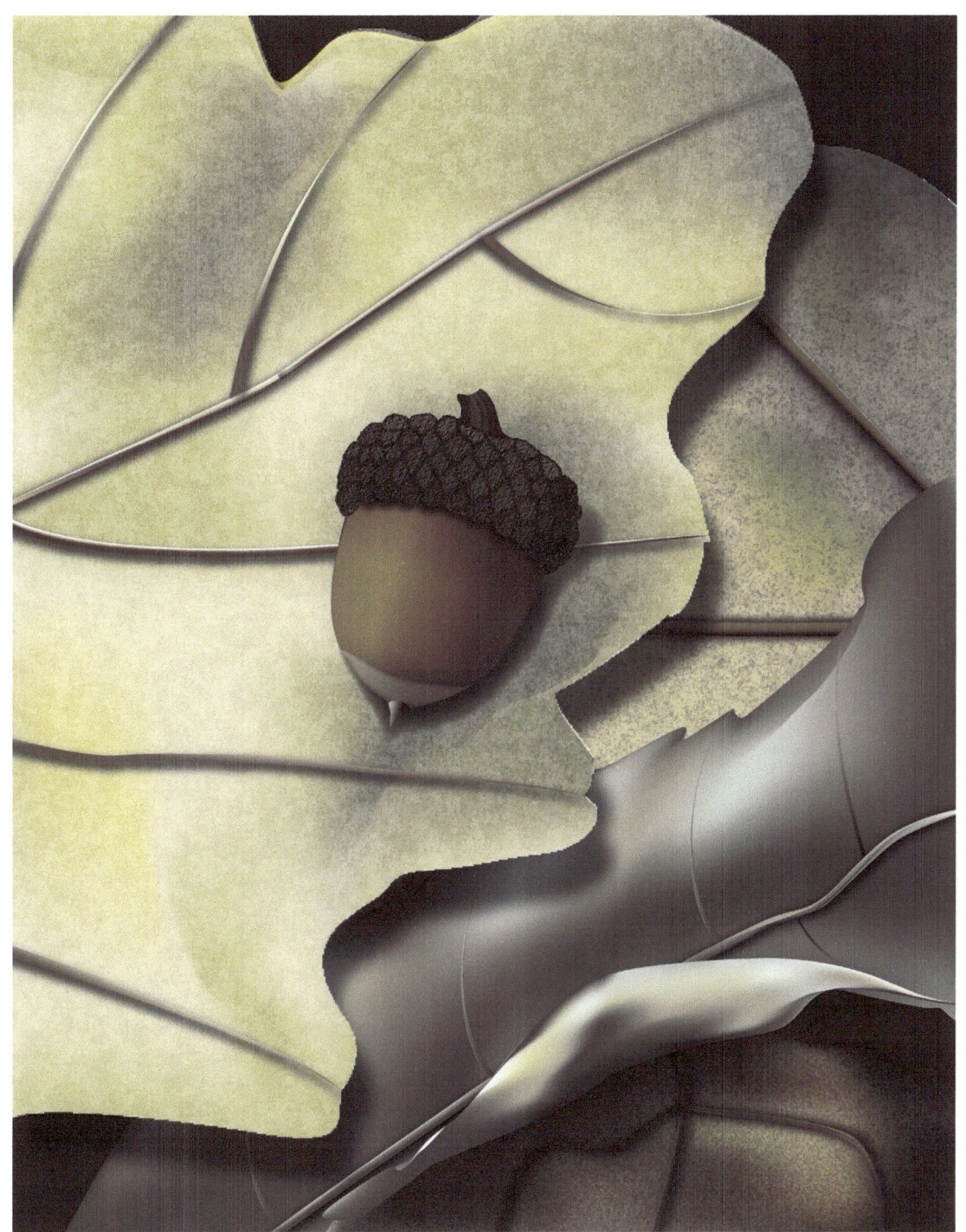

Oak Leaves Leaf

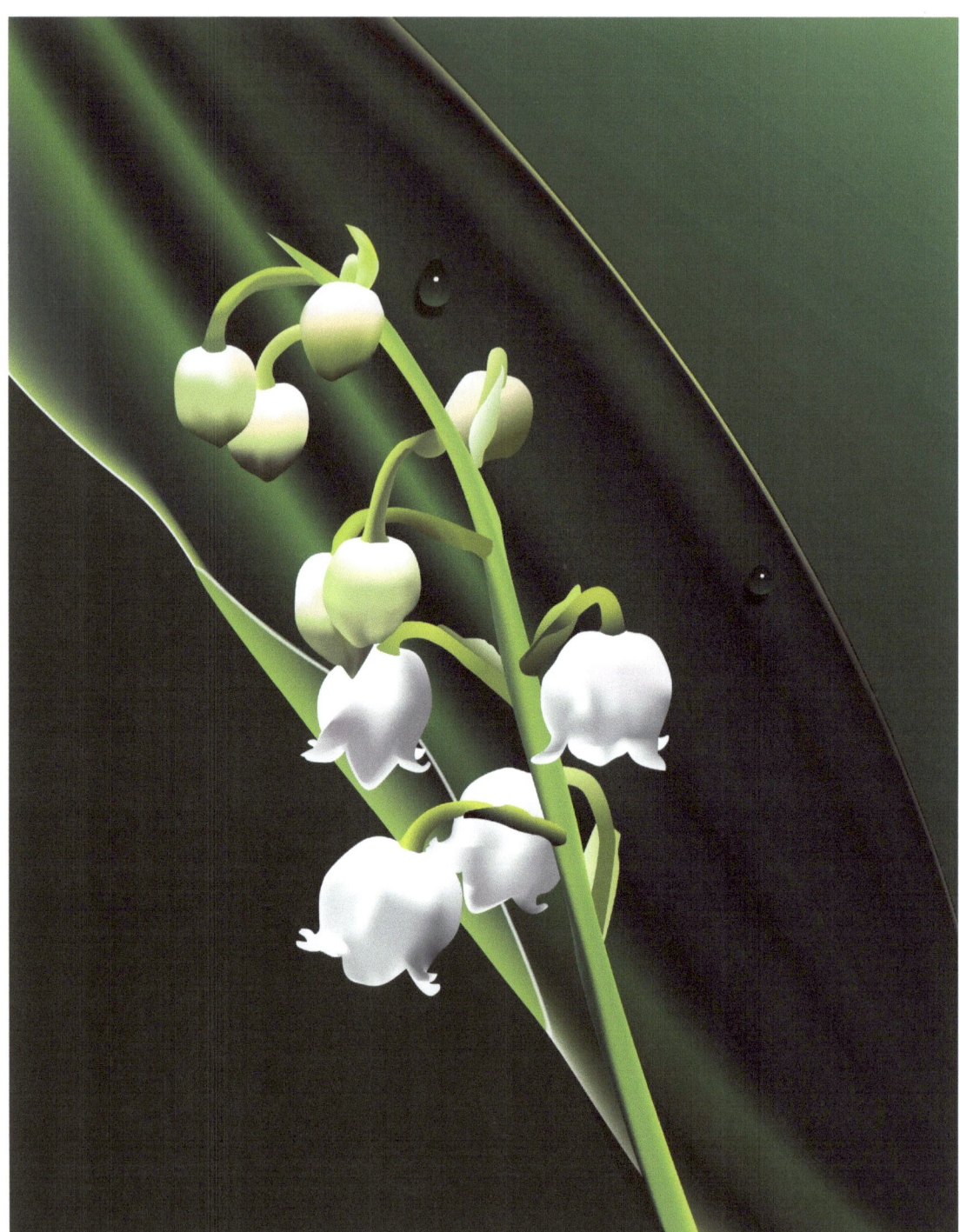

Lily of the Valley

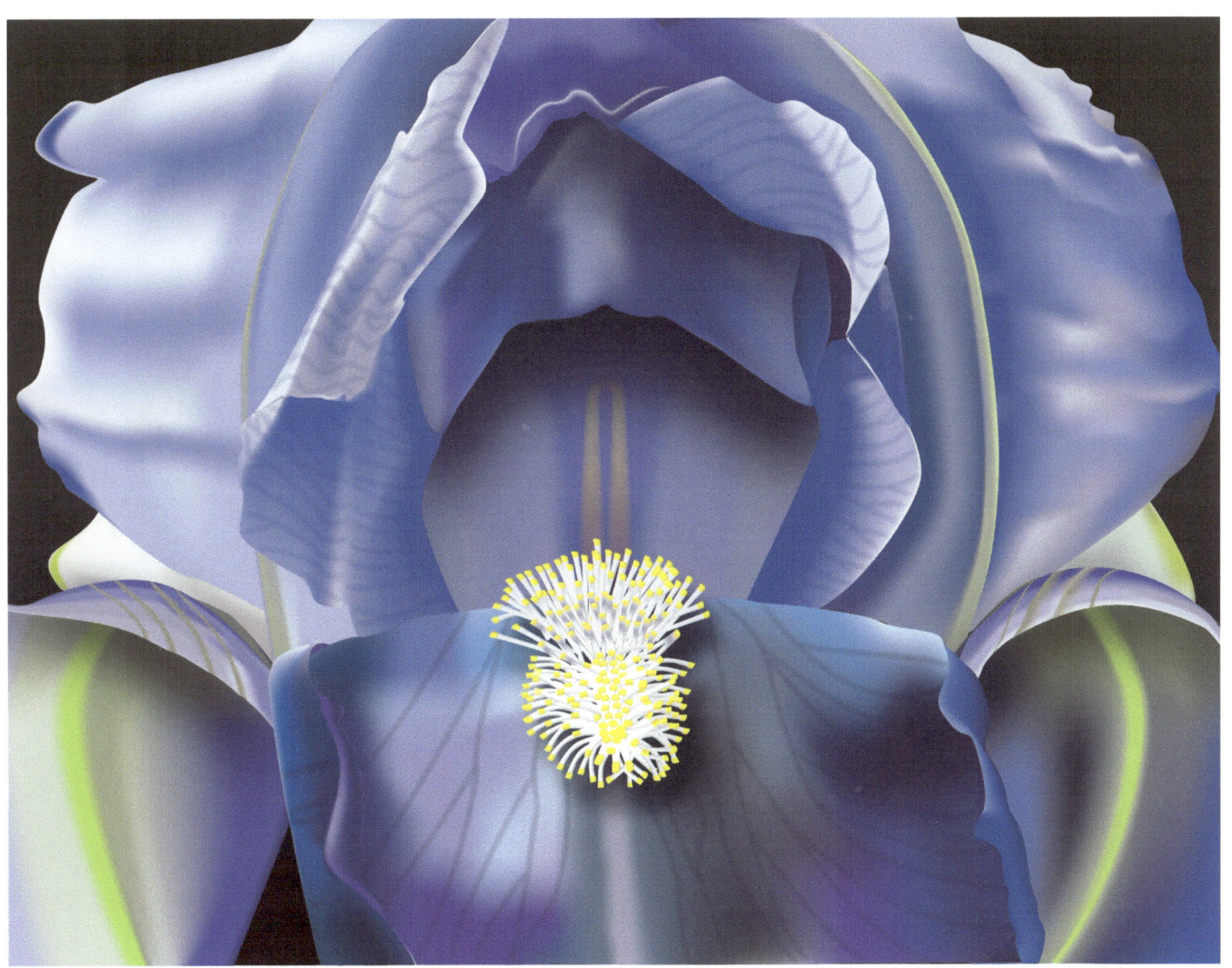

Iris

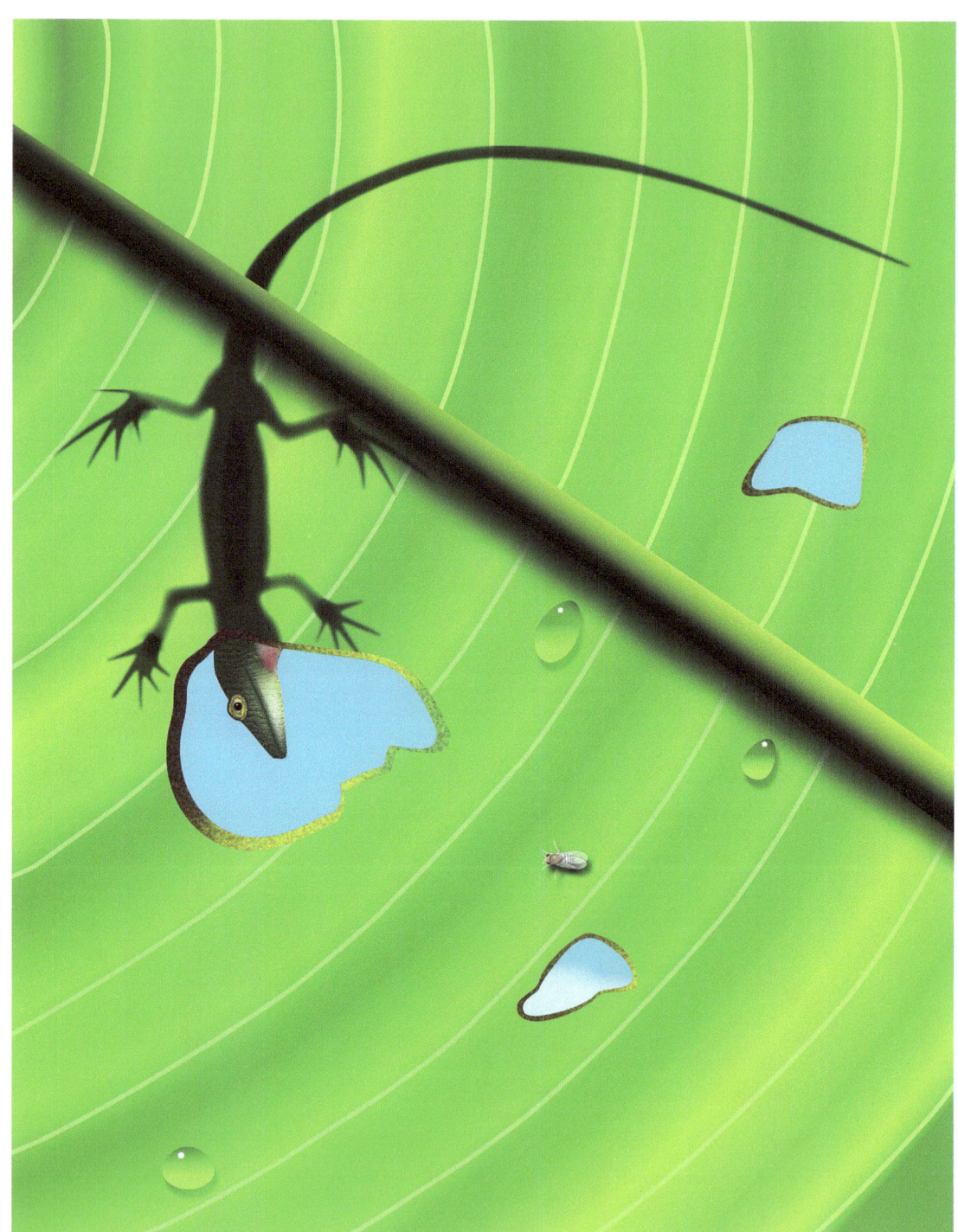

Through the Wormhole

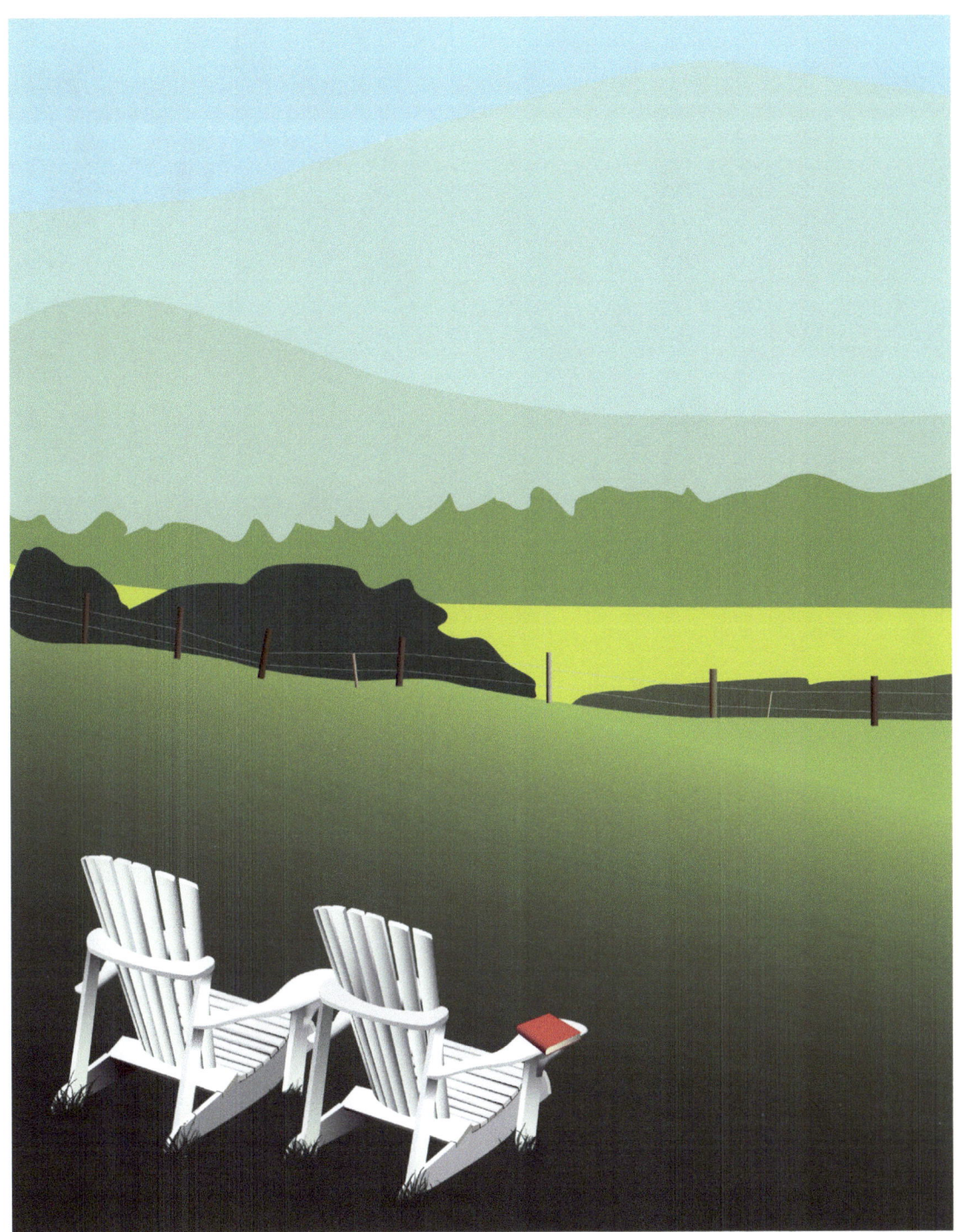

Hill Farm / Vermont

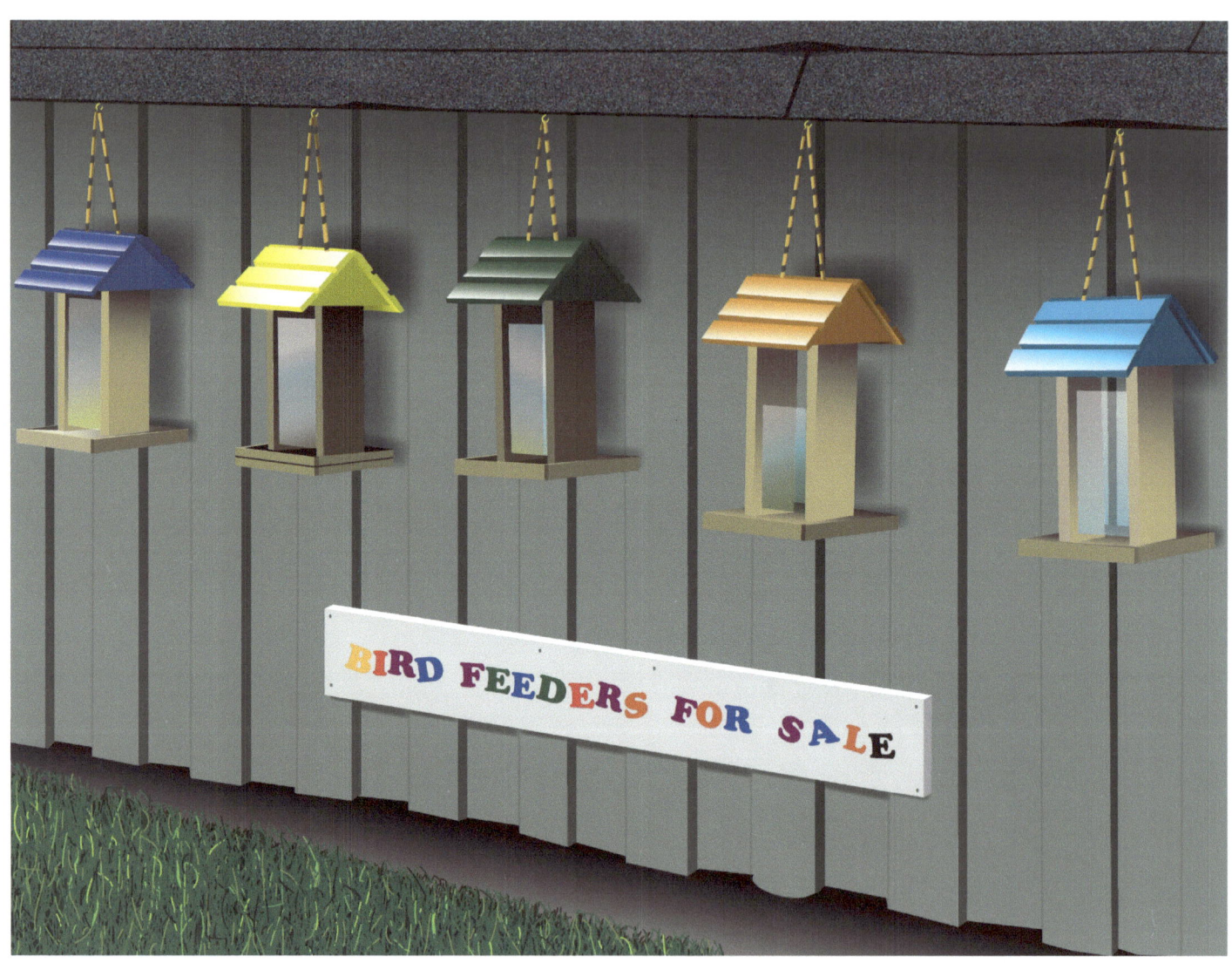

Bird Feeders / Vermont

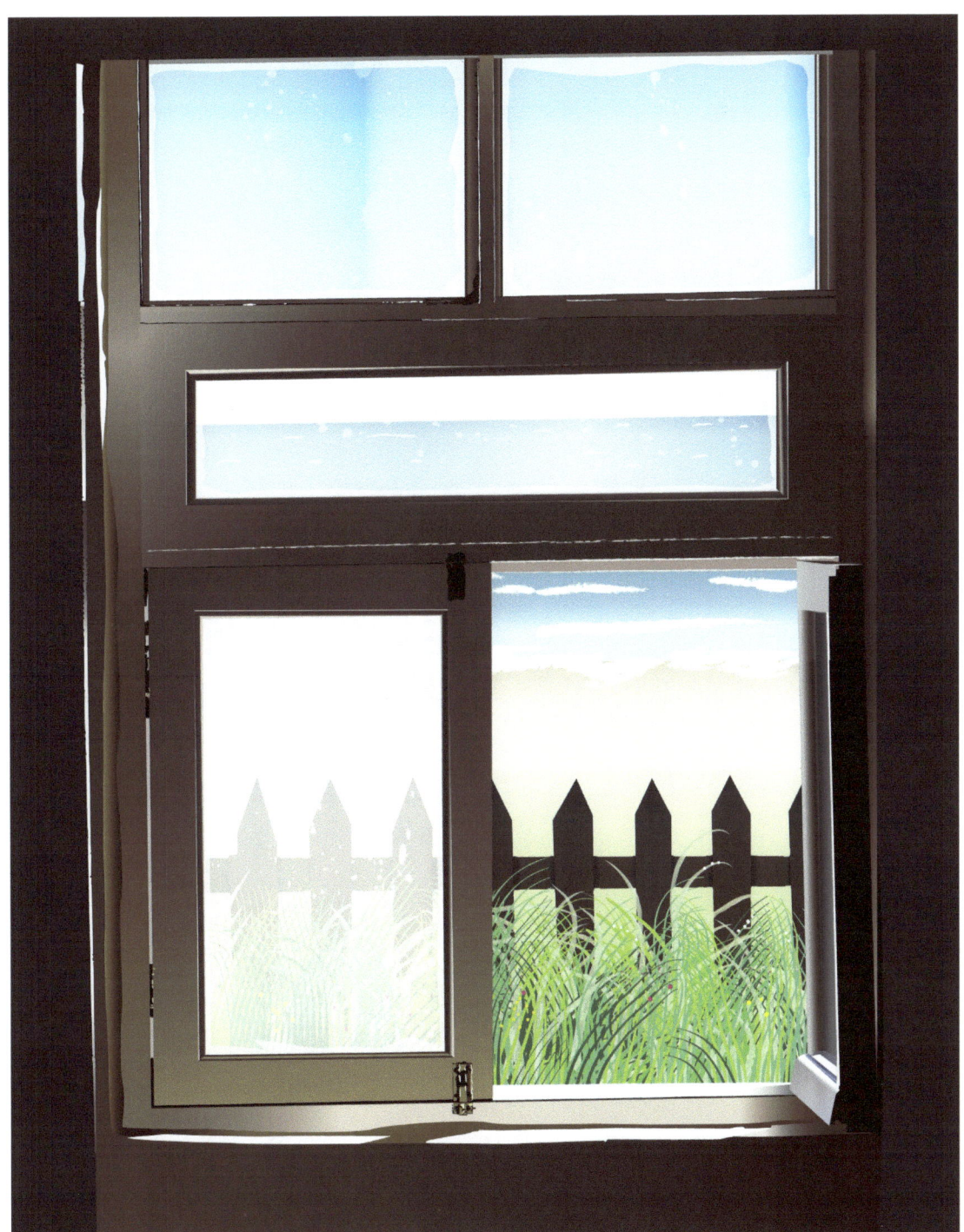

Window / Aruba

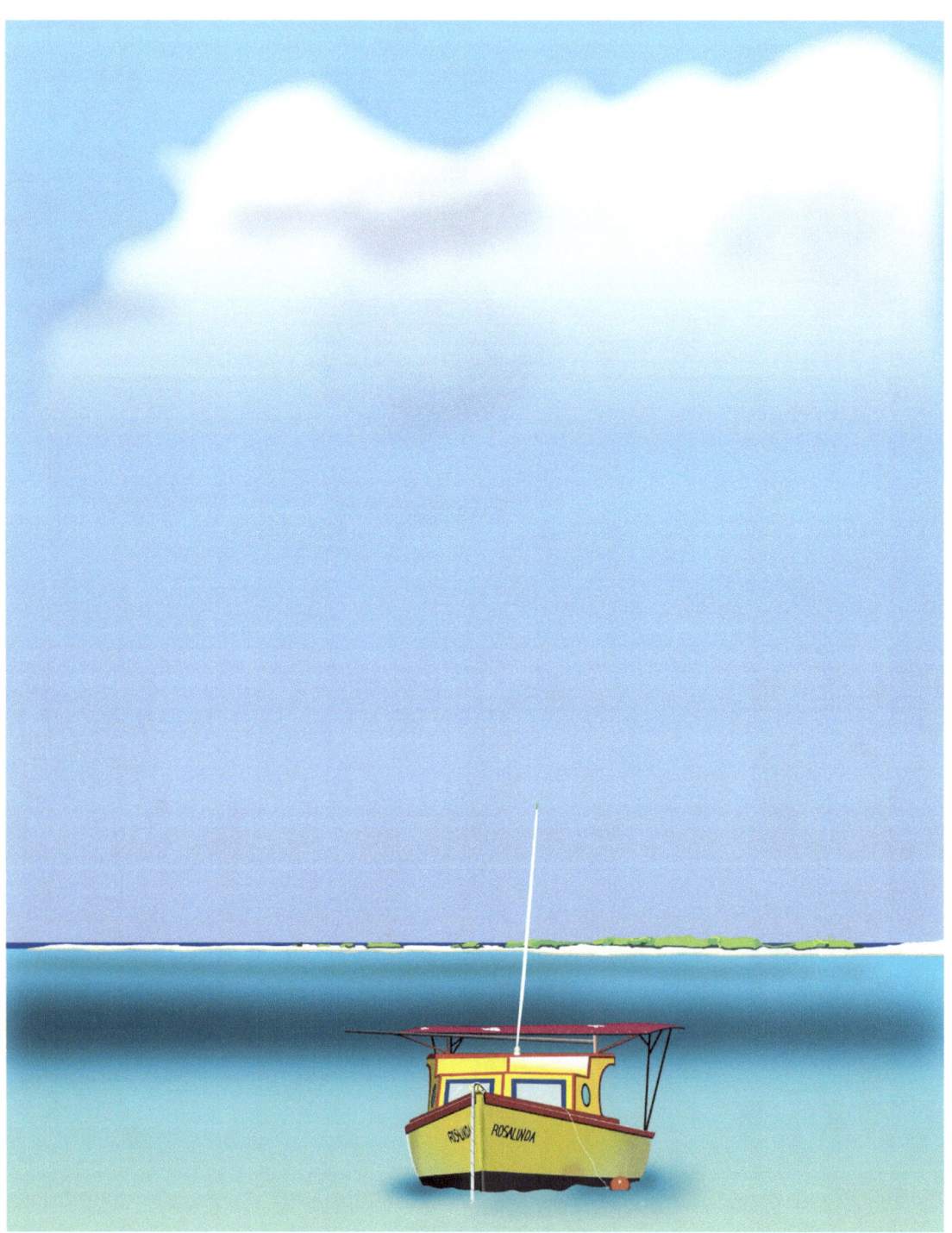

Rosalinda / Aruba

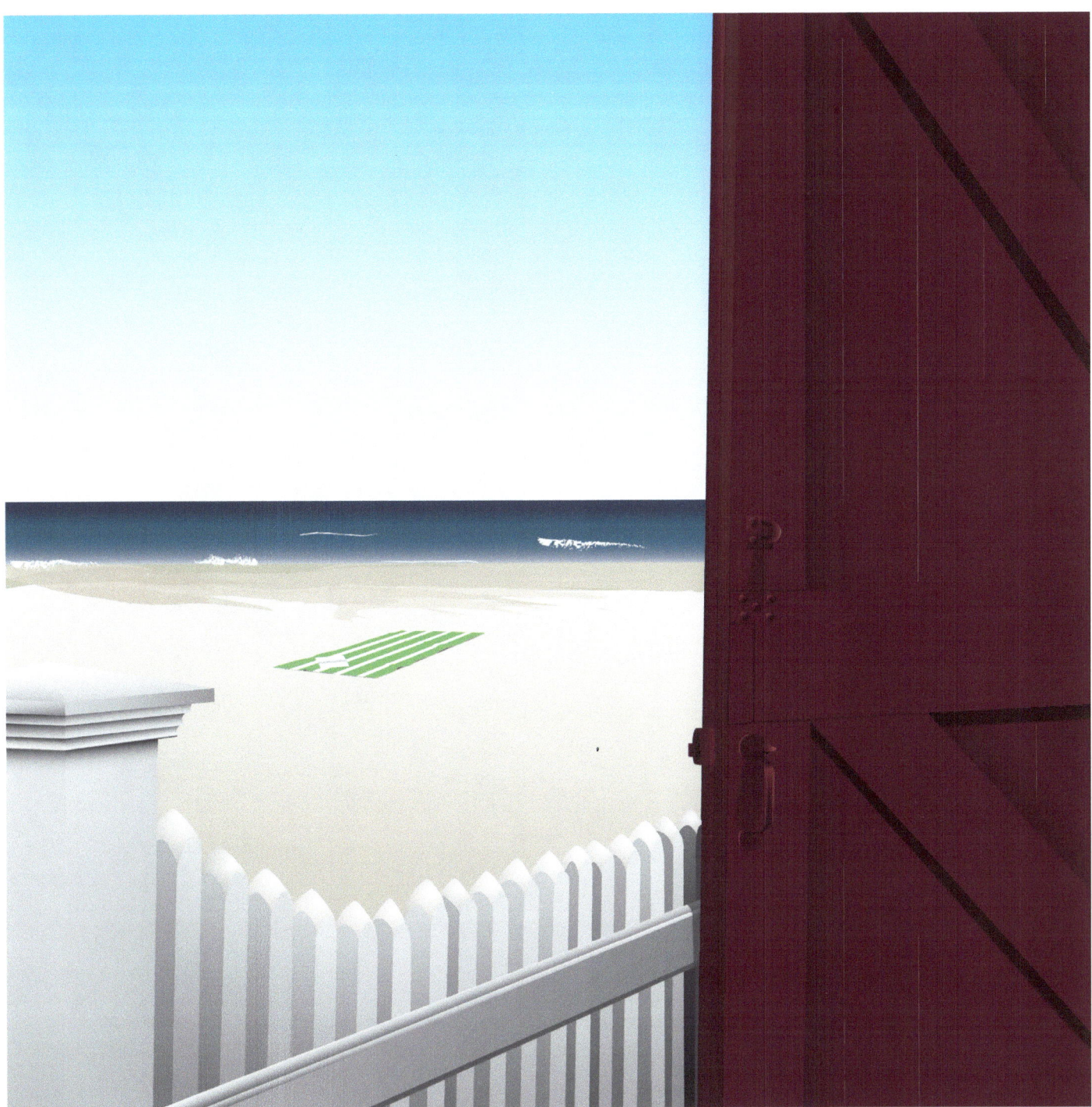

Barn Door / Provincetown

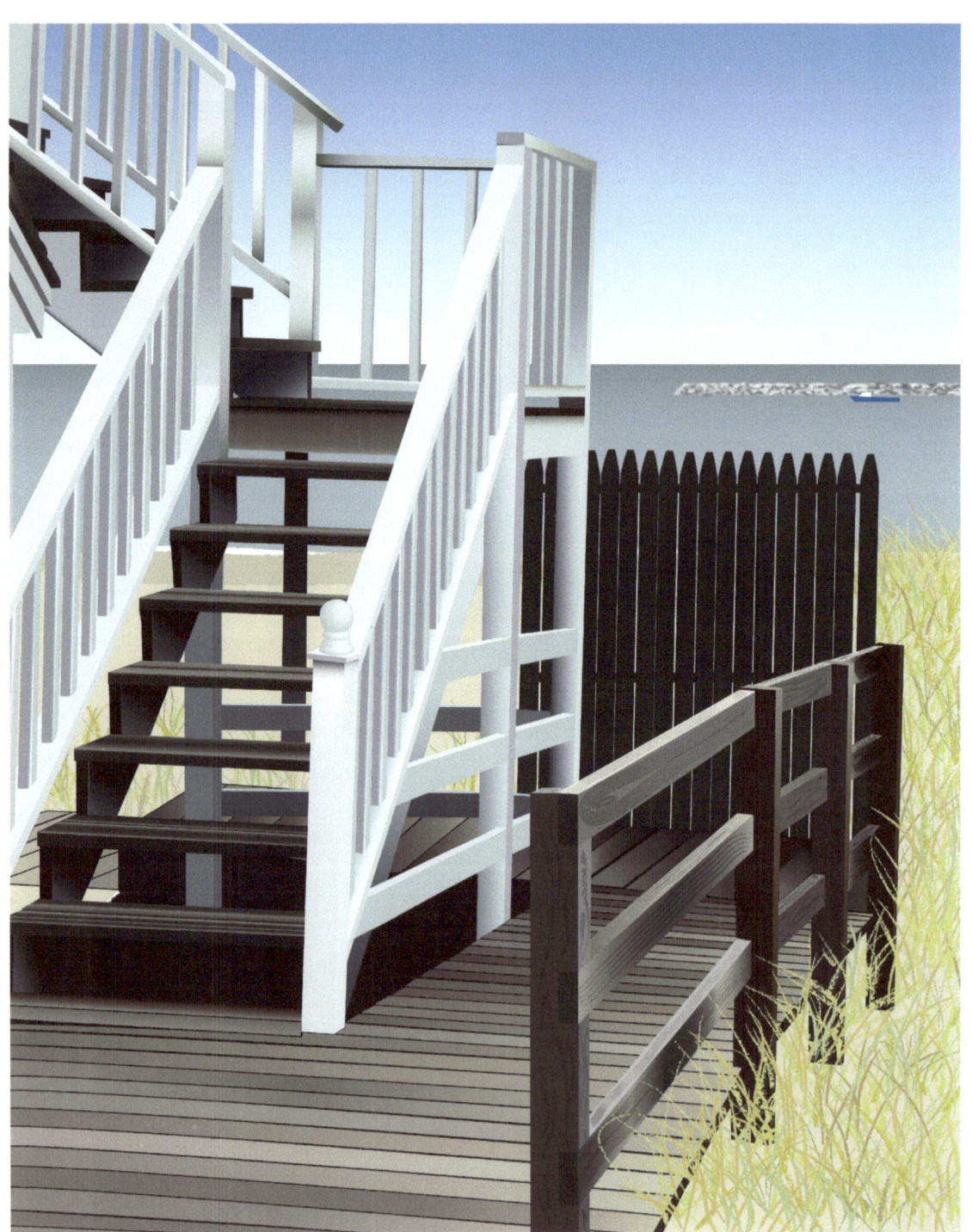

Steps / Provincetown

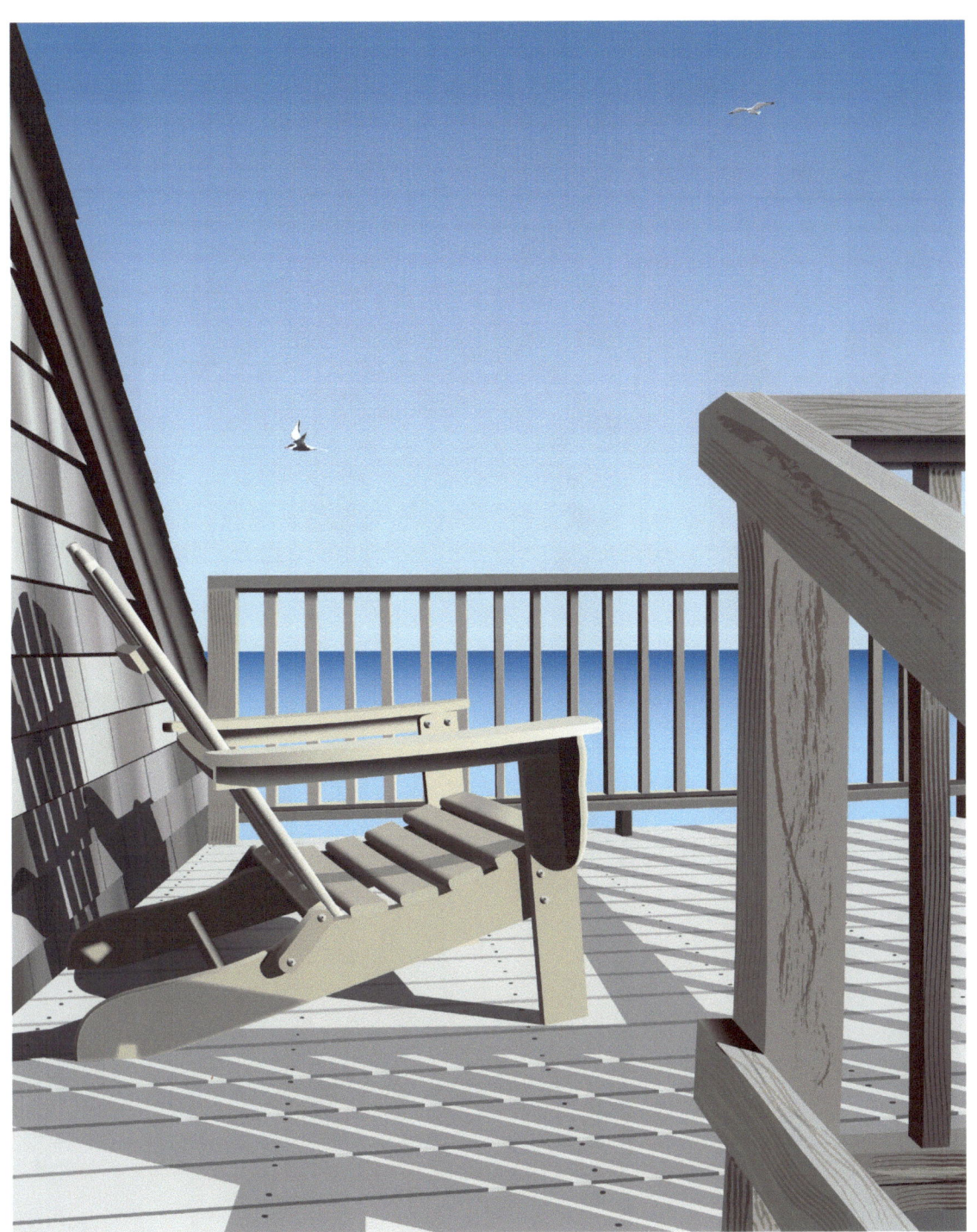

Deck / Provincetown

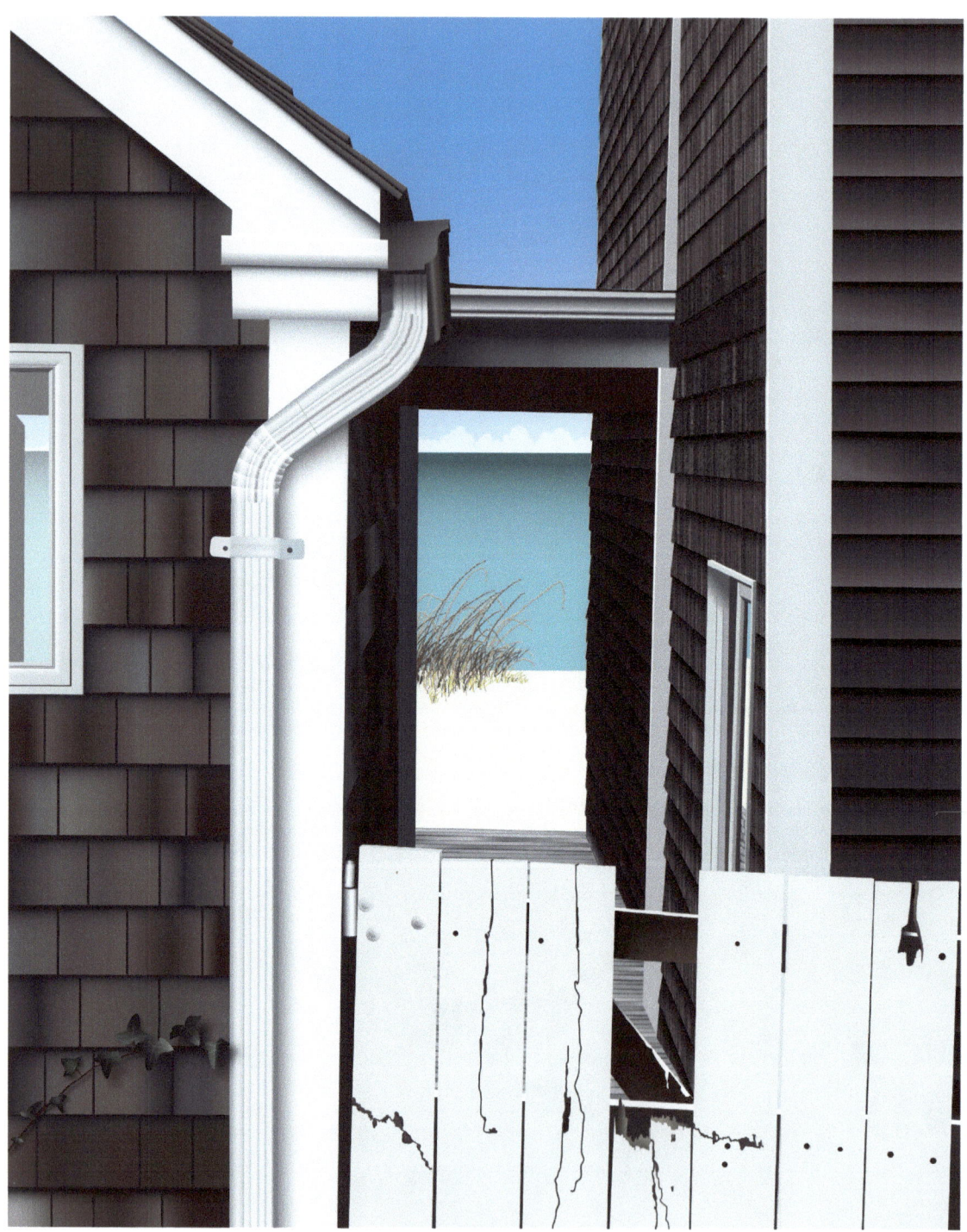

Breezeway / Provincetown

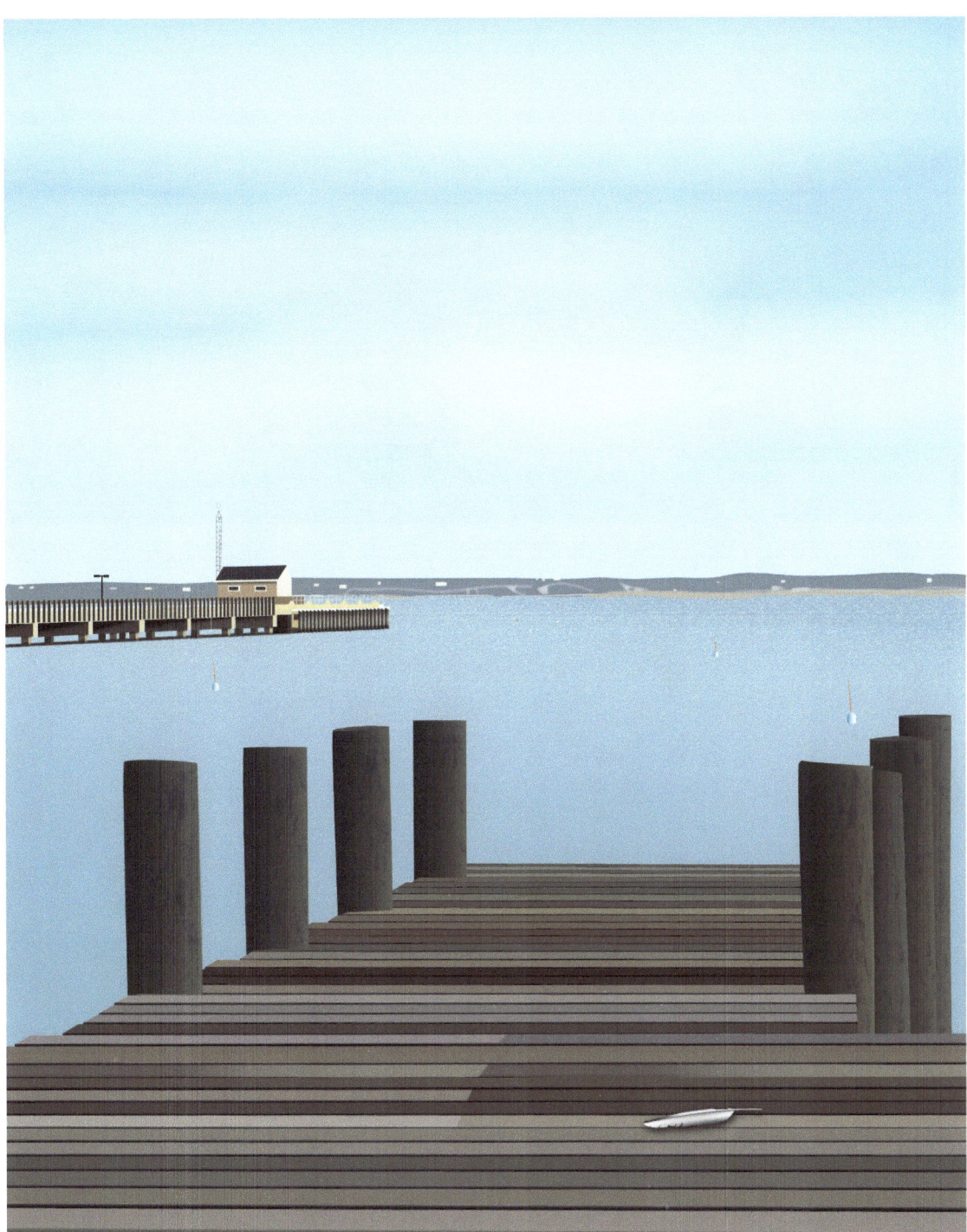

Dock / Provincetown

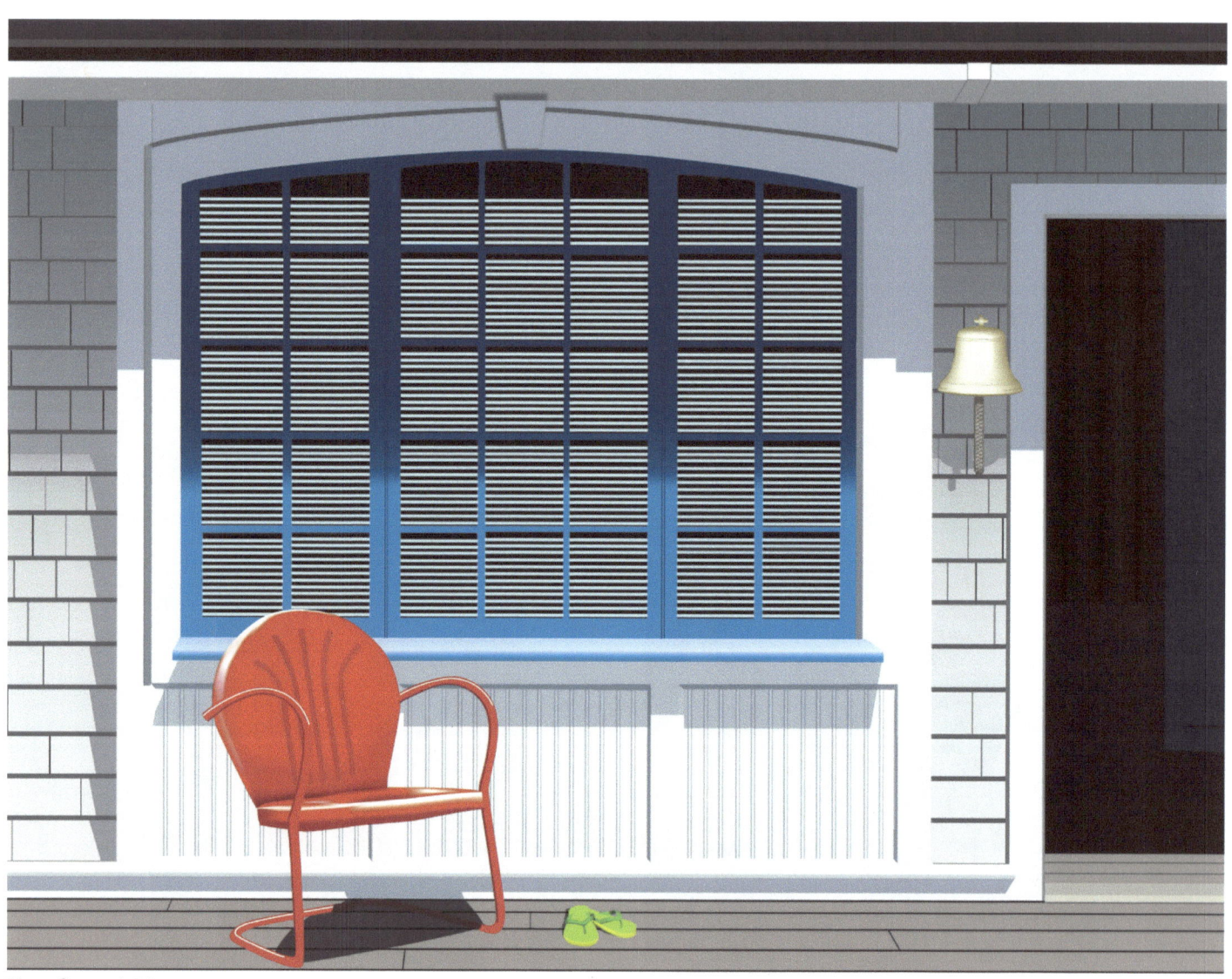

Flop-flops / Gloucester

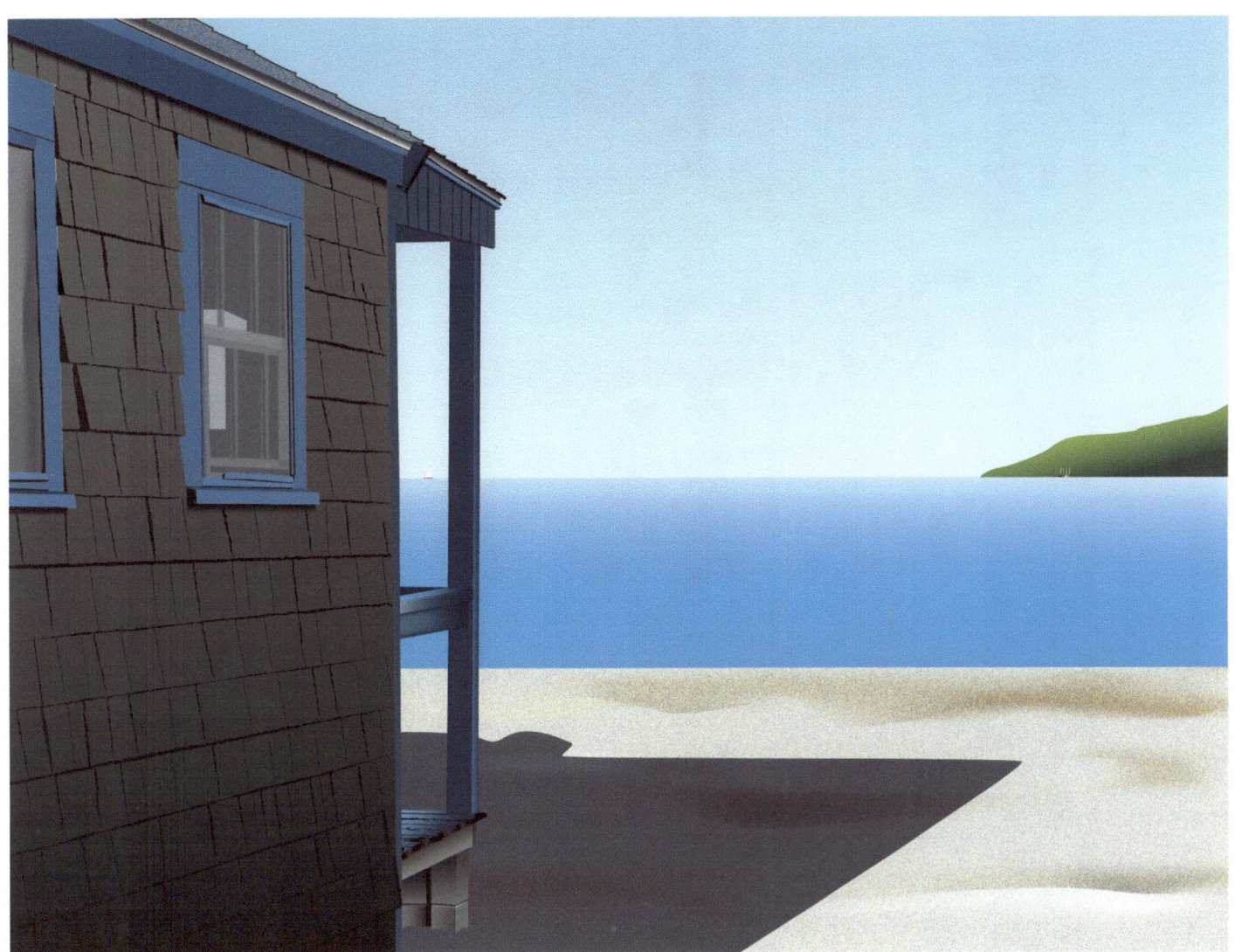

Shack / Gloucester

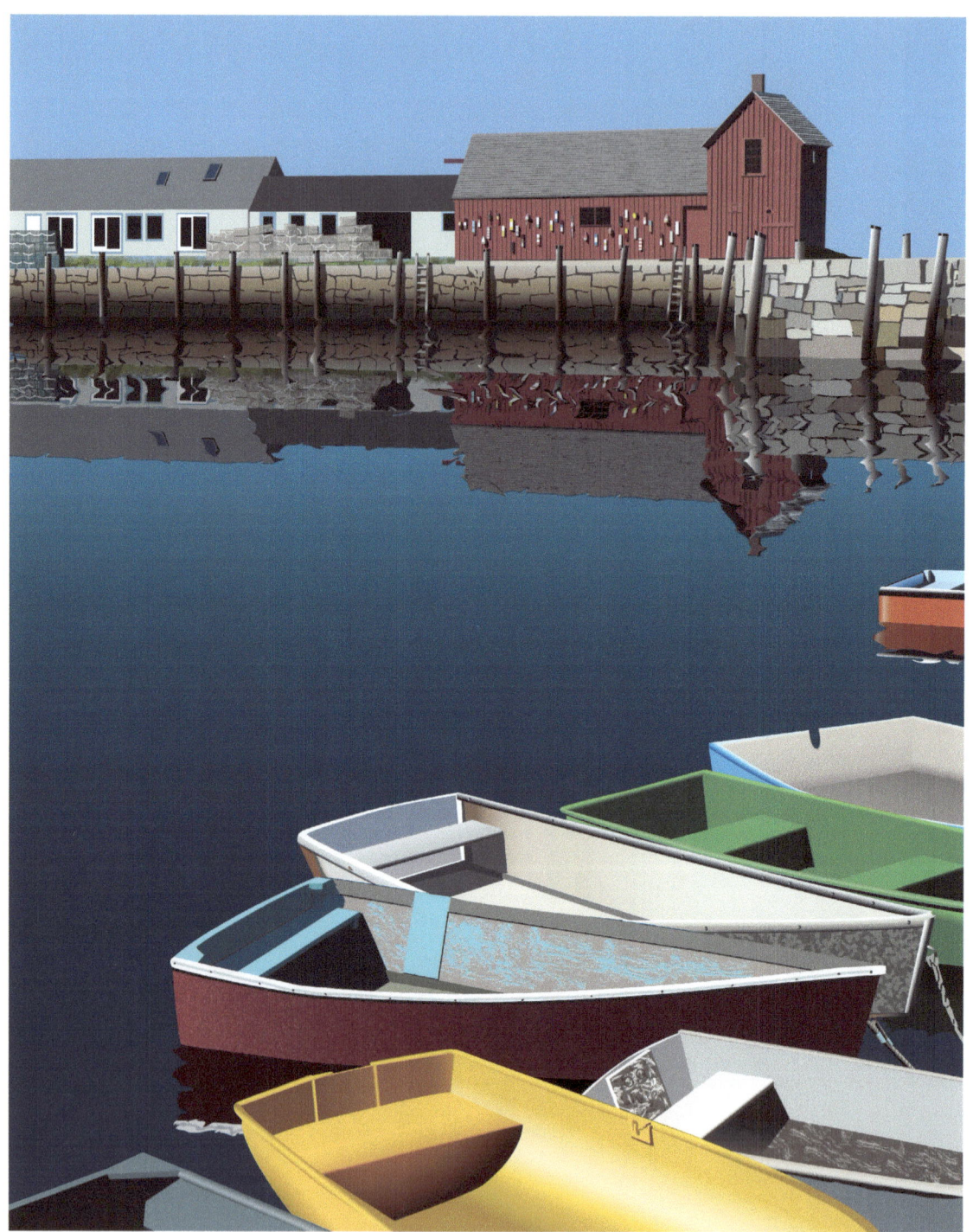

Motif / Rockport

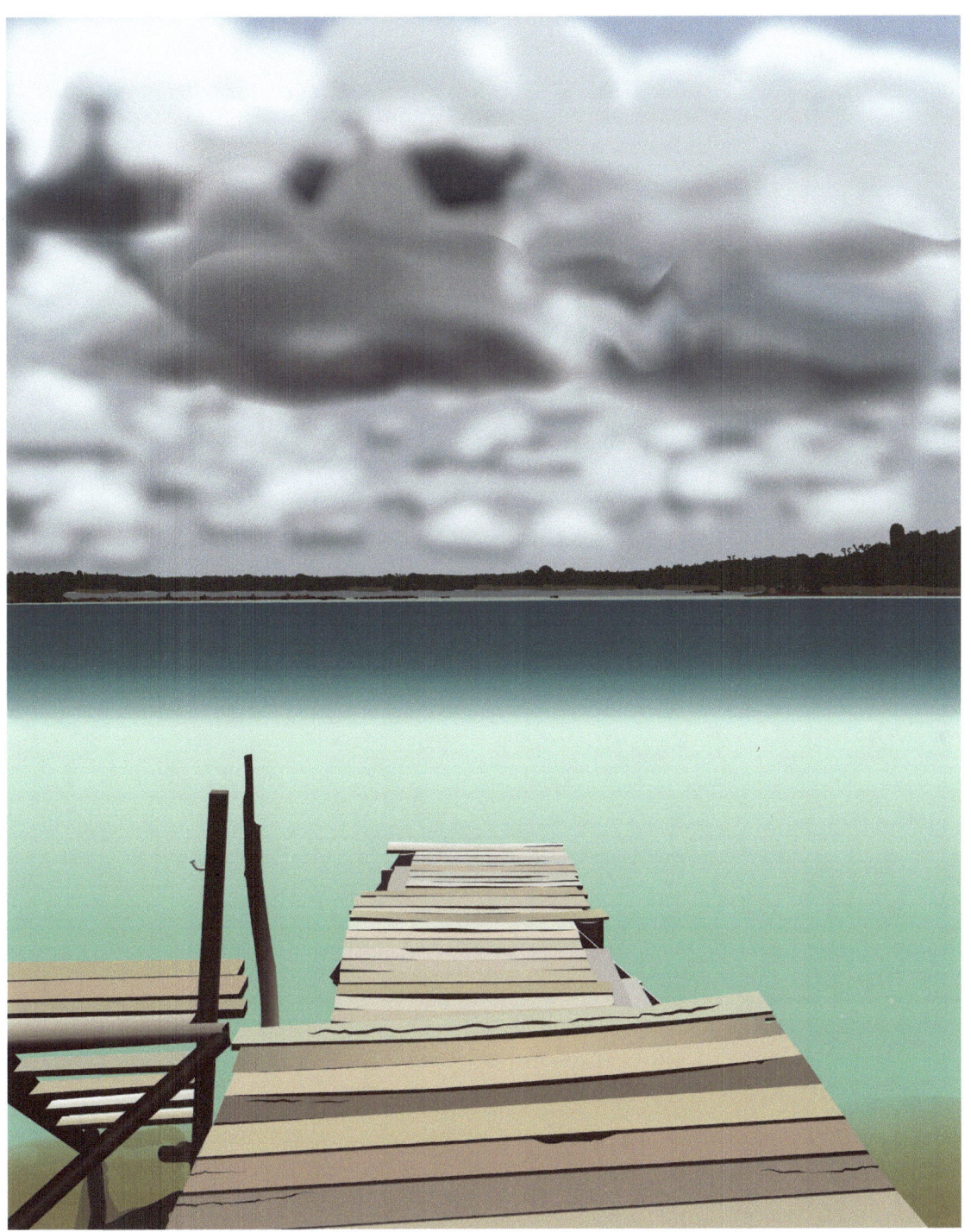

Dock / Yucatan

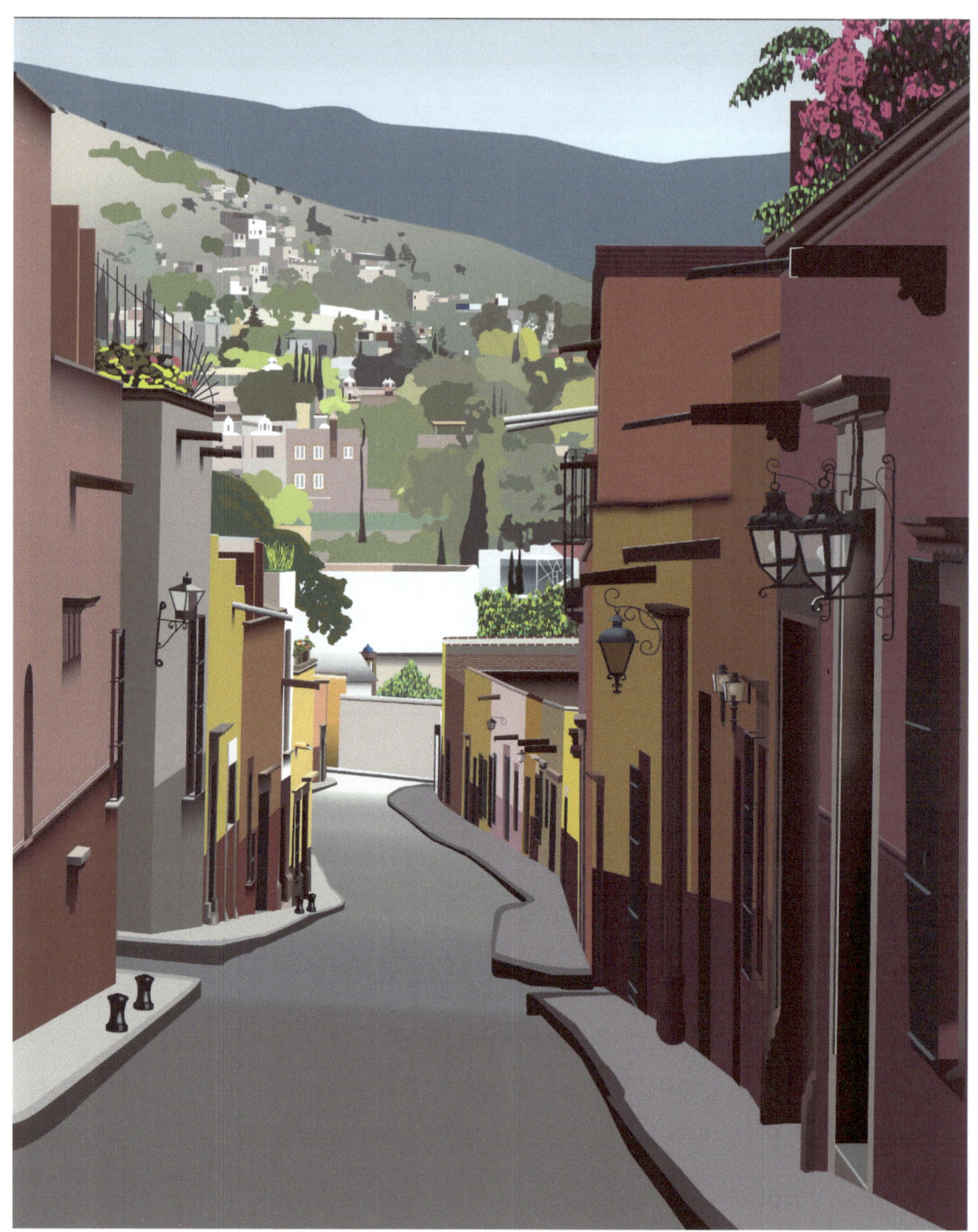

Calle de Jesus / San Miguel de Allende

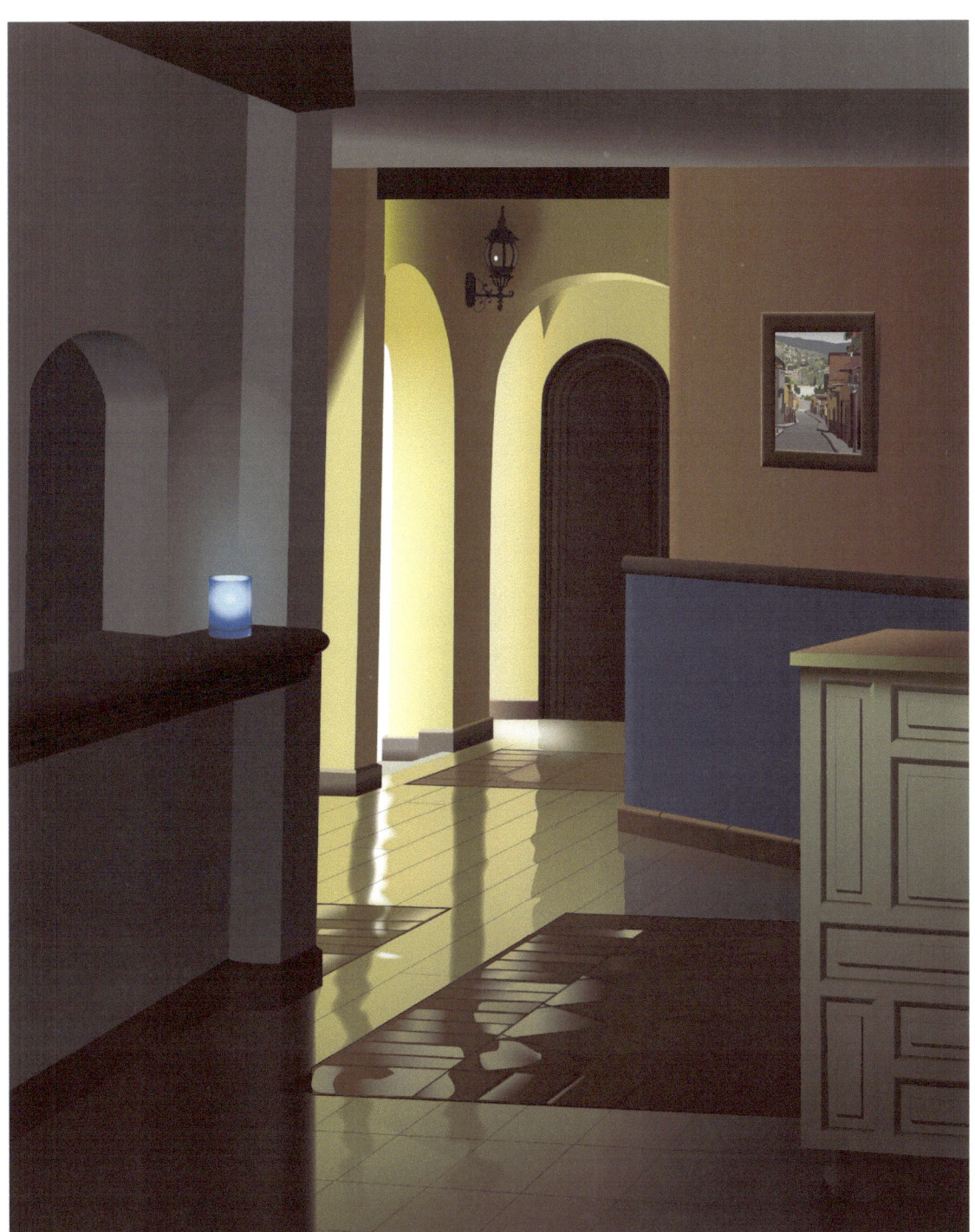

Lobby / San Miguel de Allende

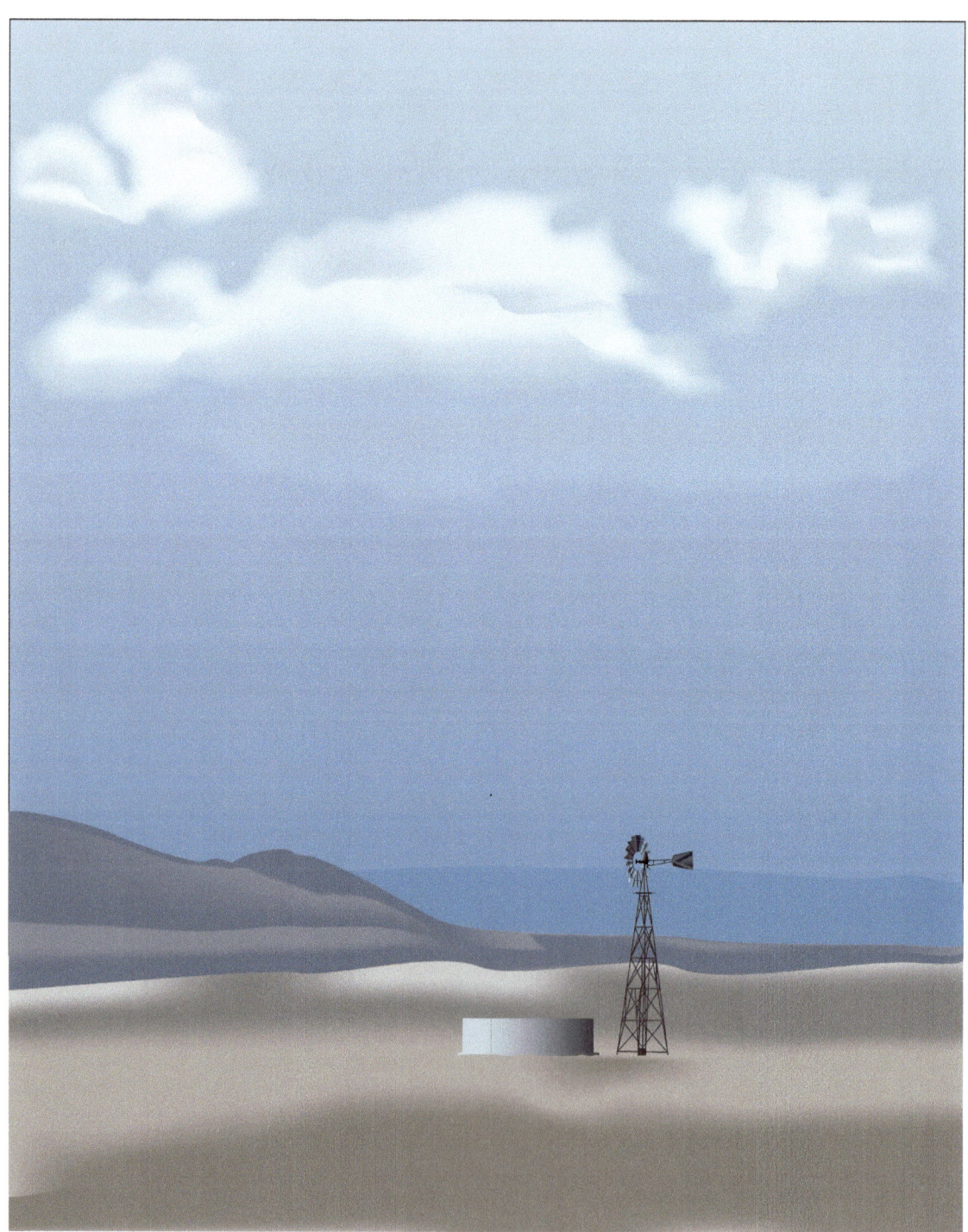

Windmill / Arizona

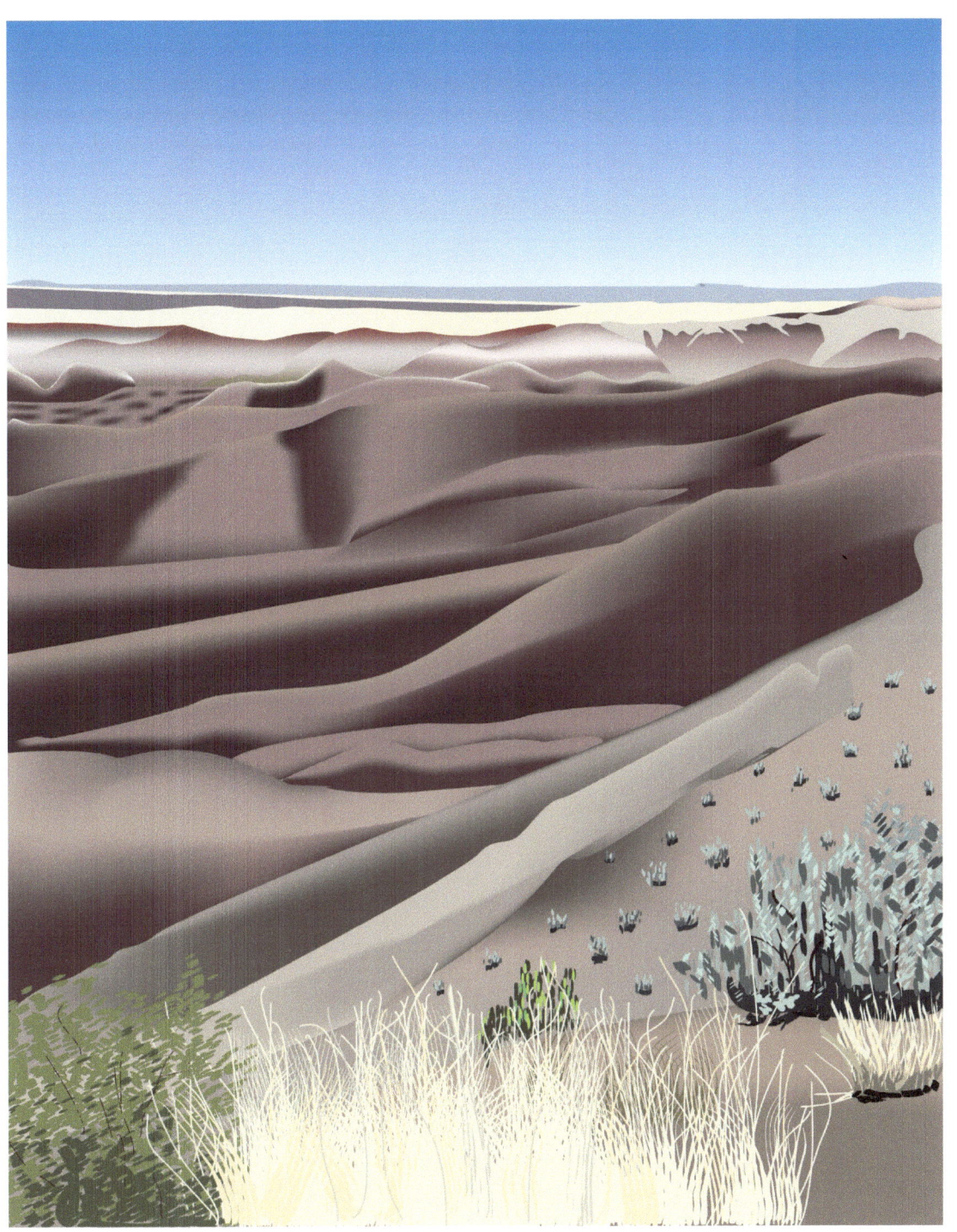

Terrain / Arizona

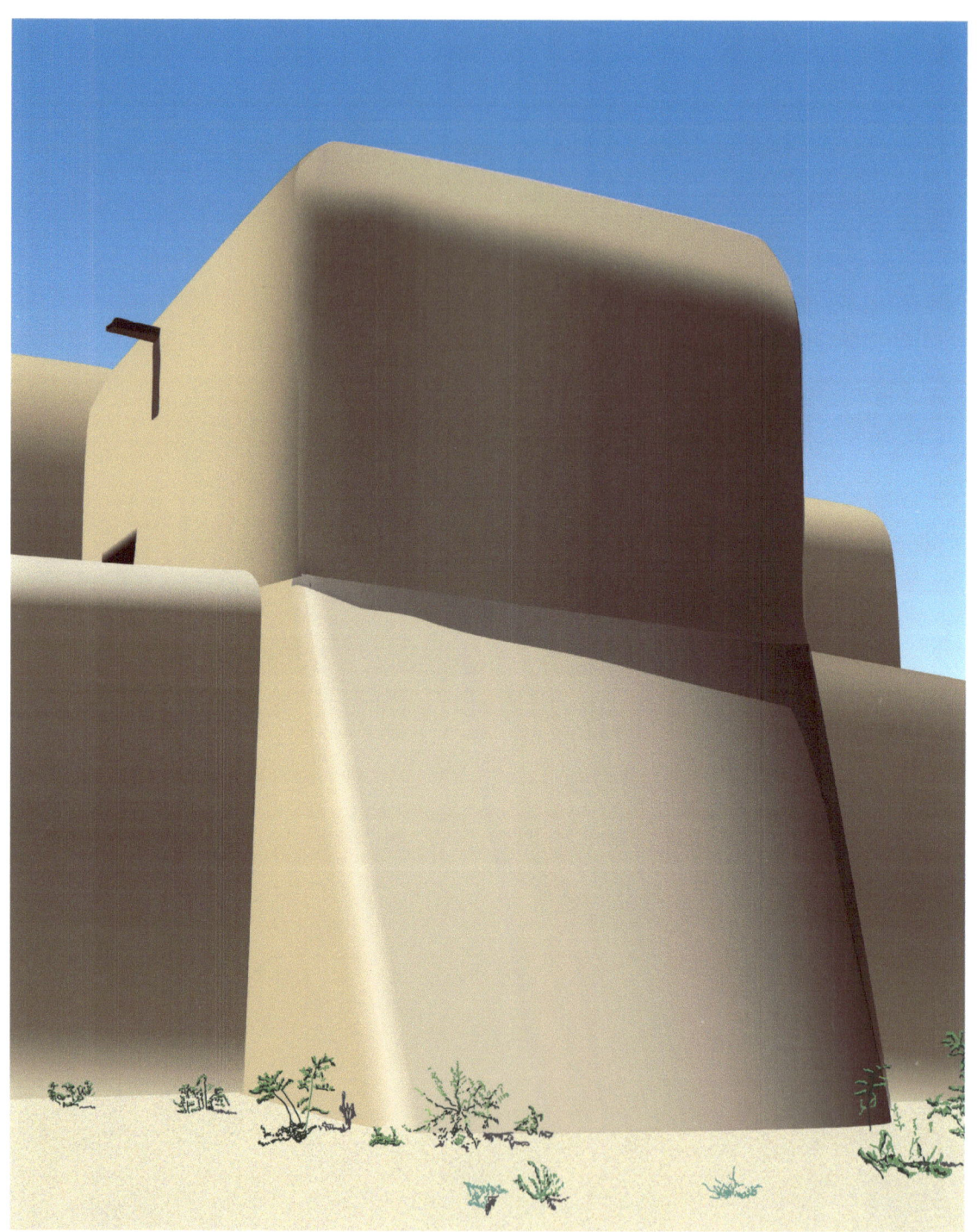

Church / Abiquiu

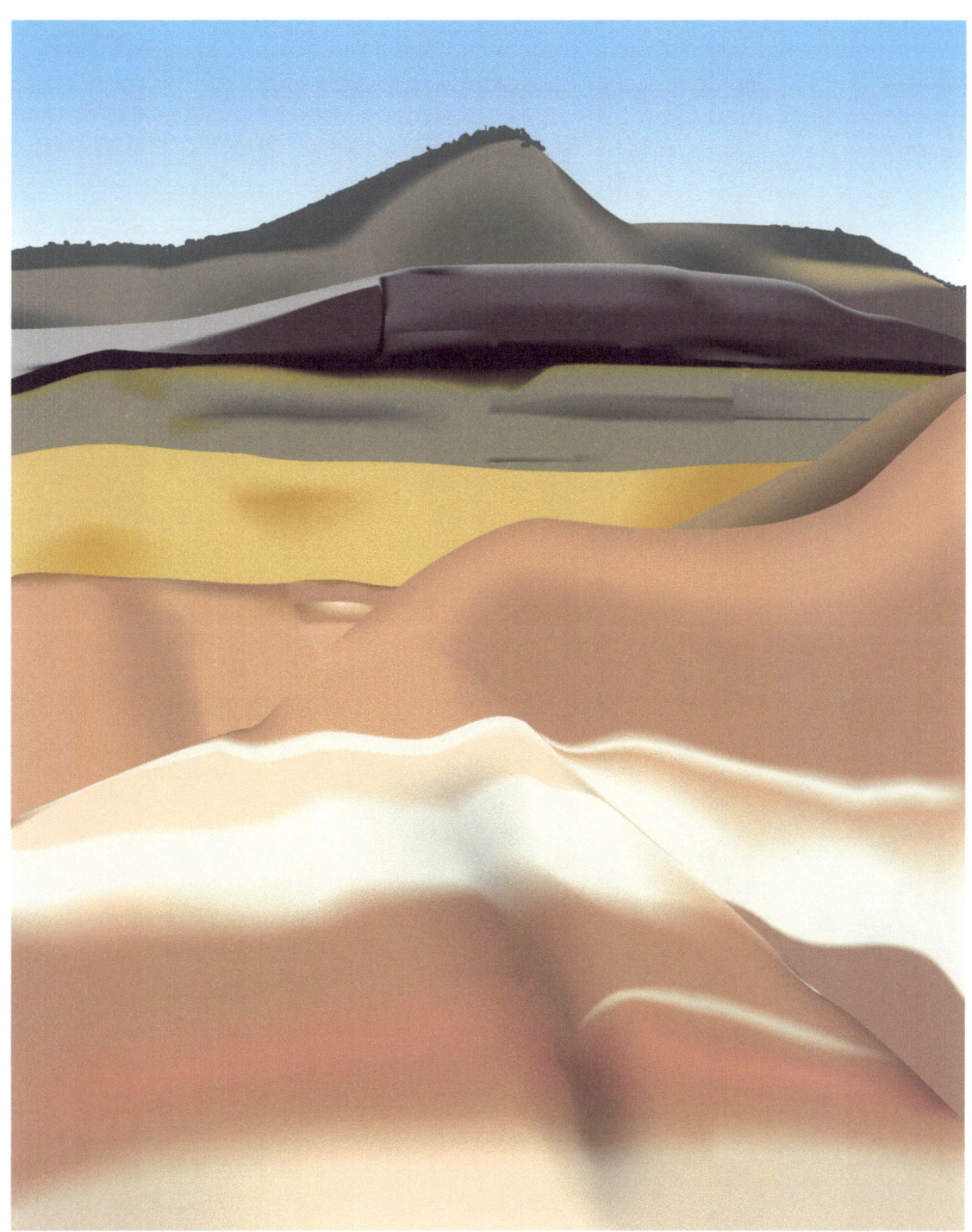

Ghost Ranch / Abiquiu

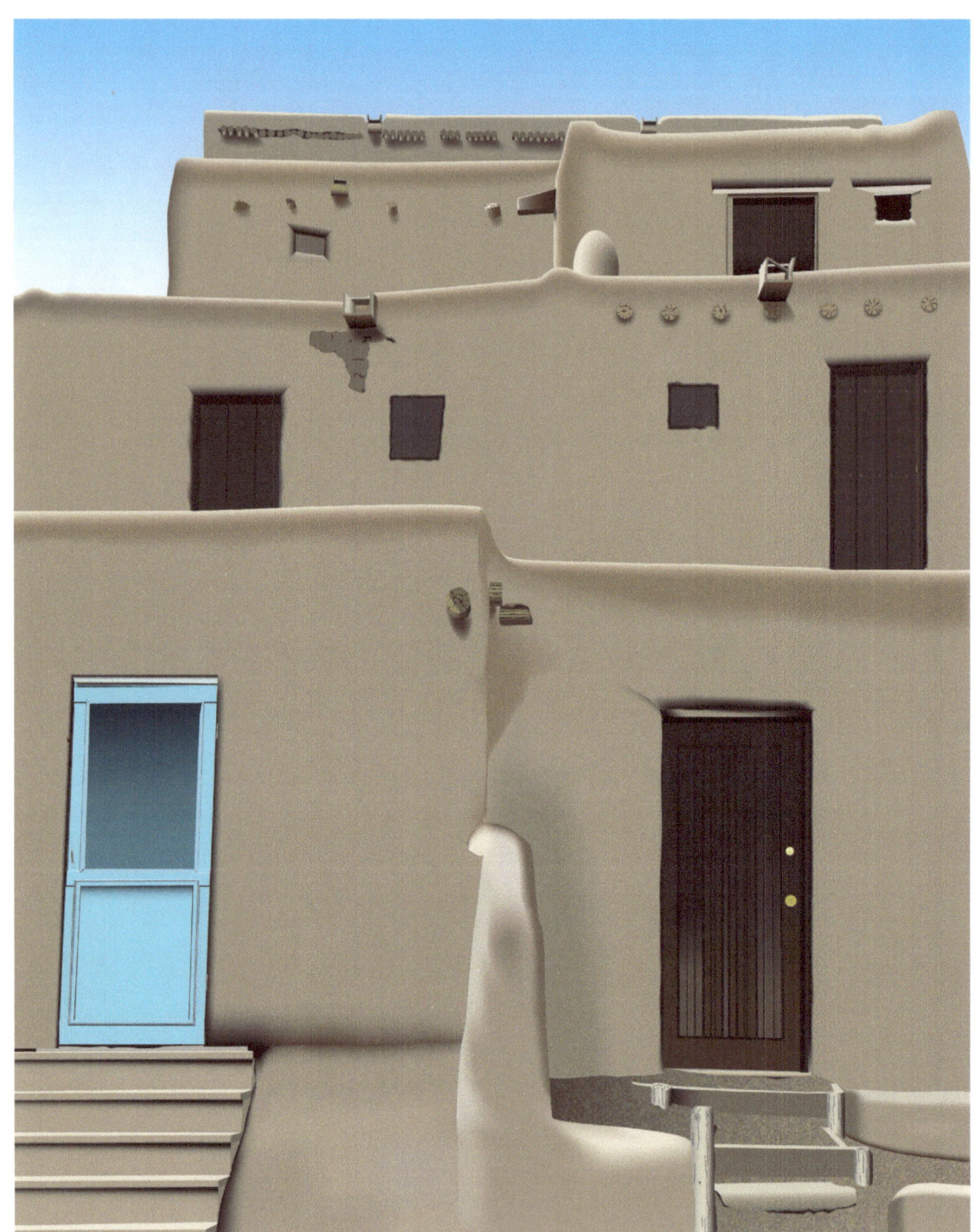

Dwellings / Taos Pueblo

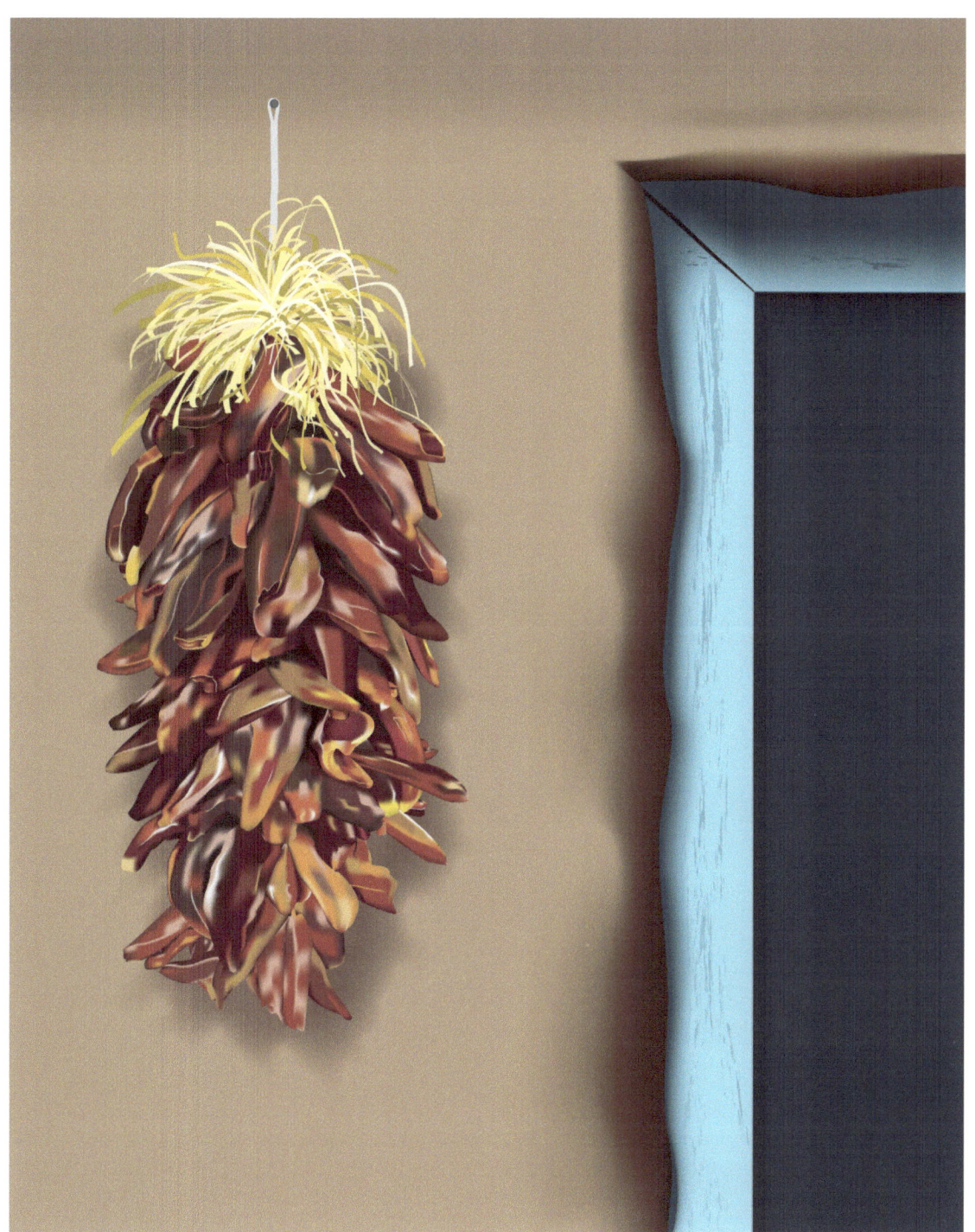

Ristra / Taos Pueblo

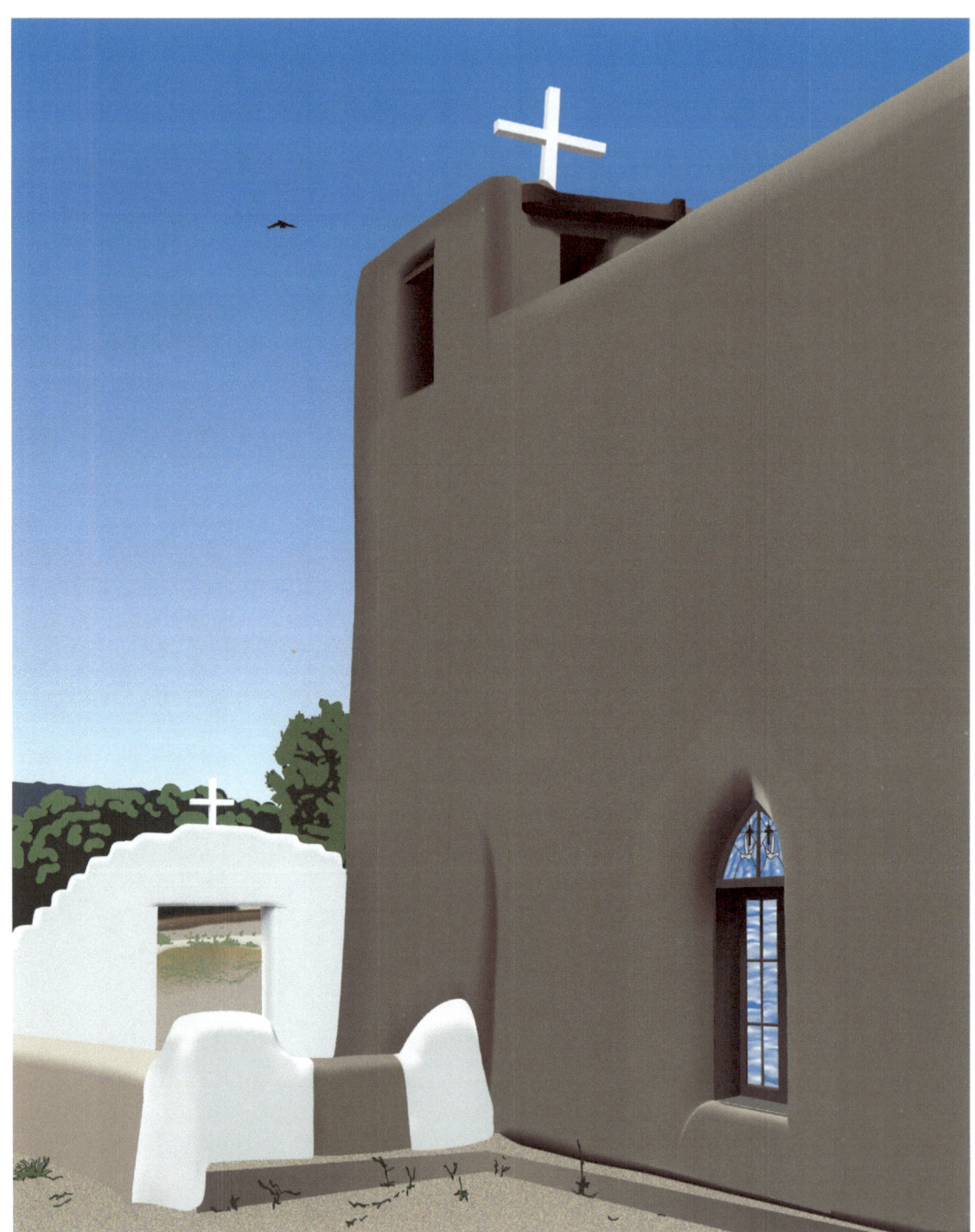

Church / Taos Pueblo

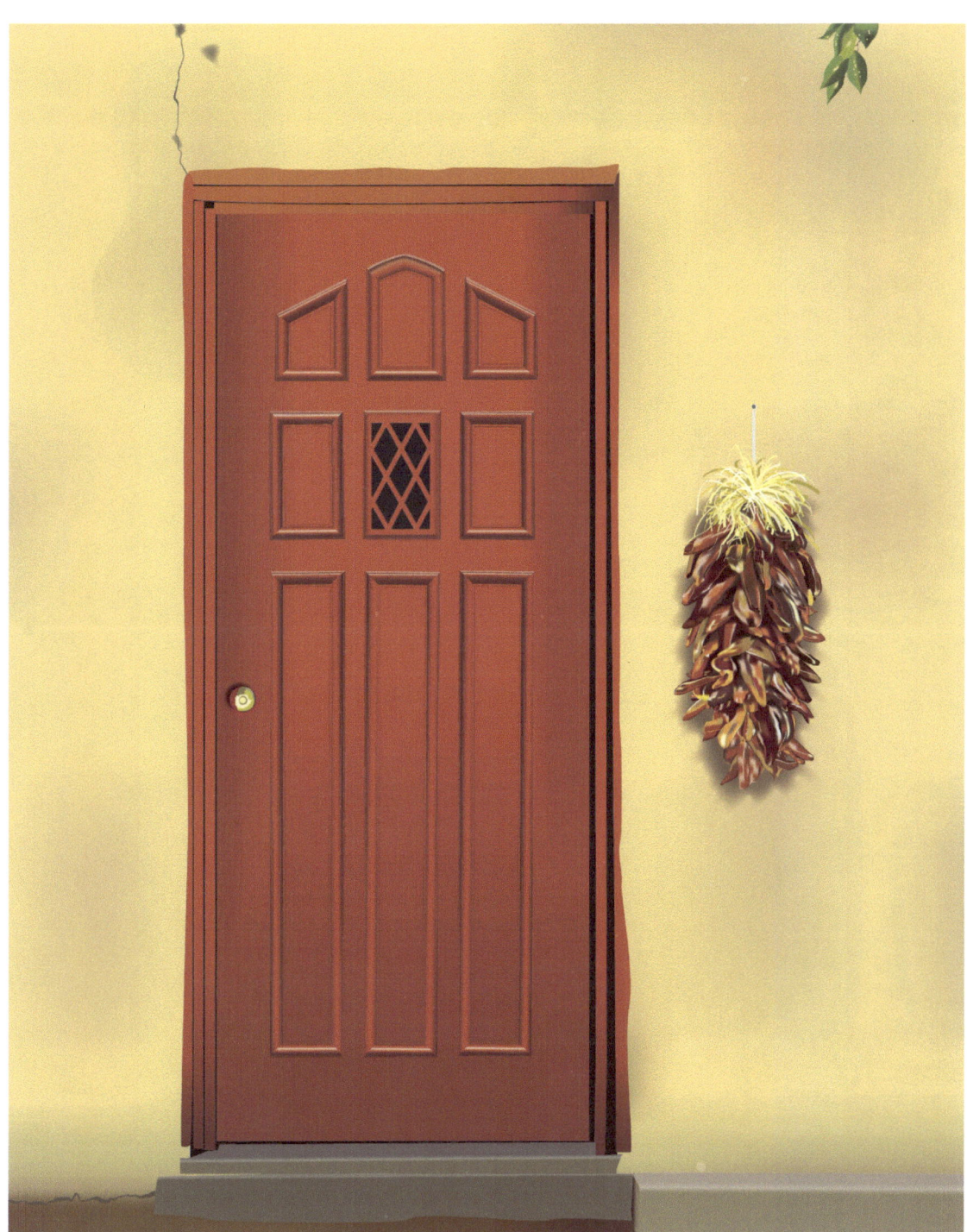

Door / Taos Pueblo

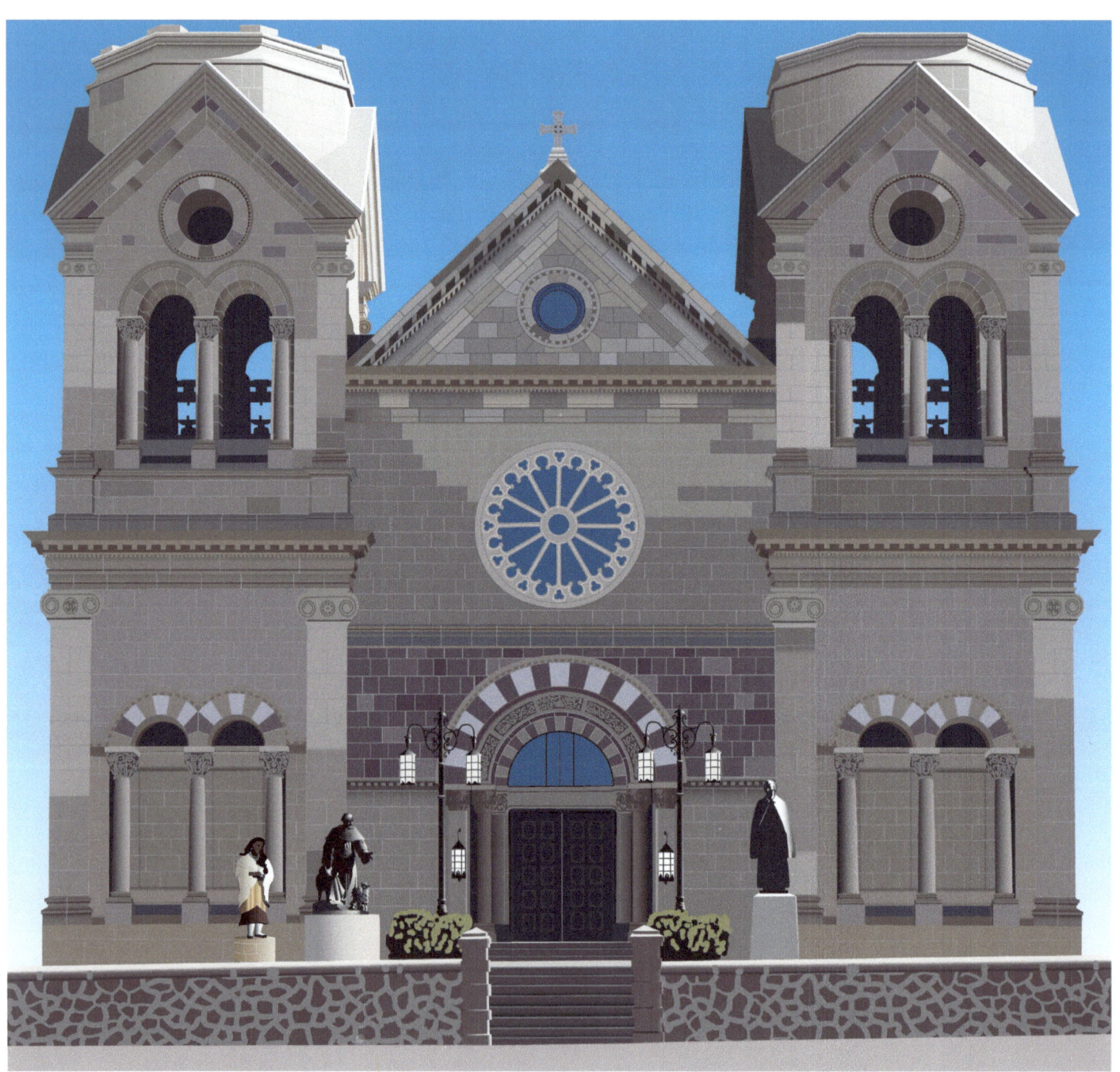

Basilica / Santa Fe

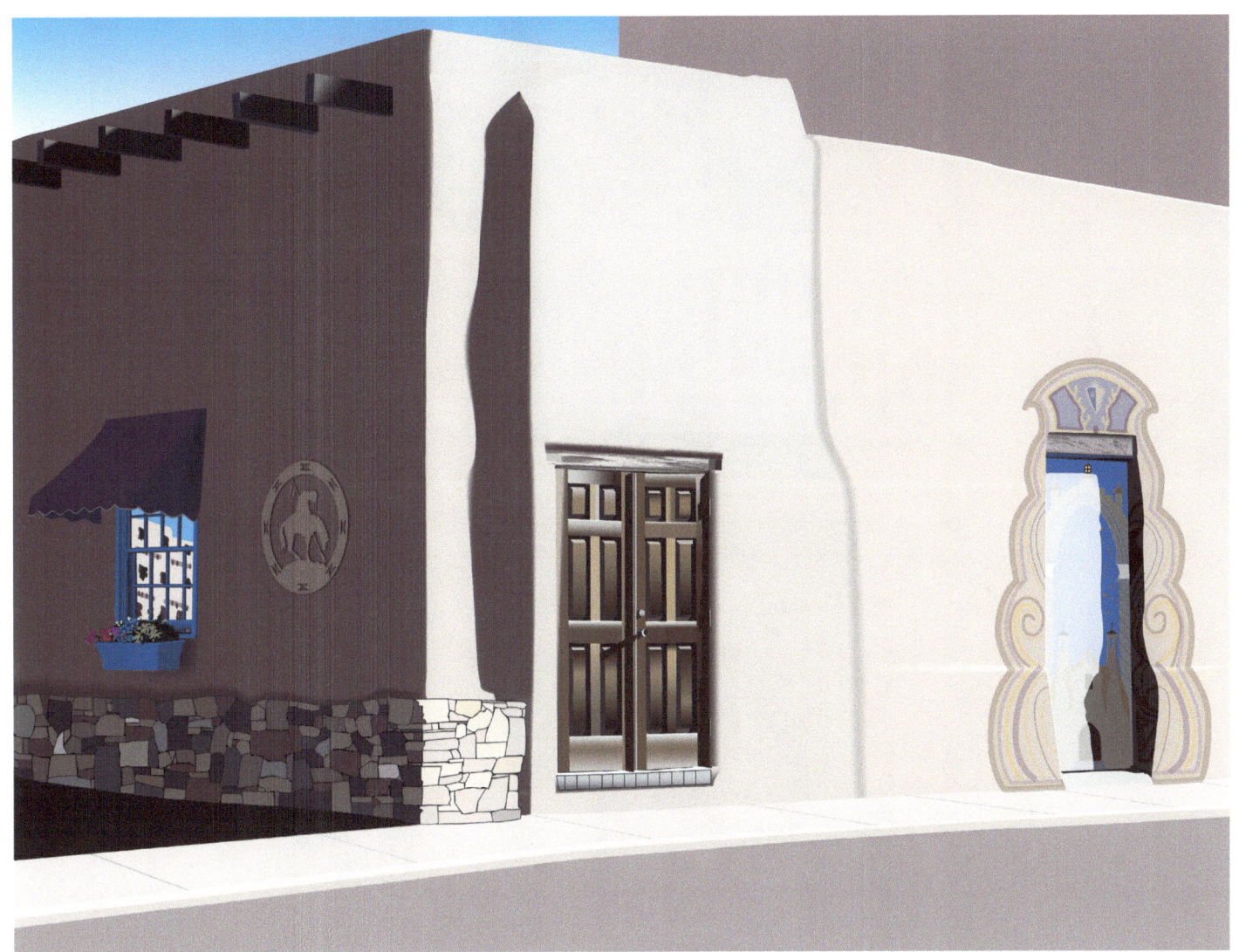

Shop 1 / Santa Fe

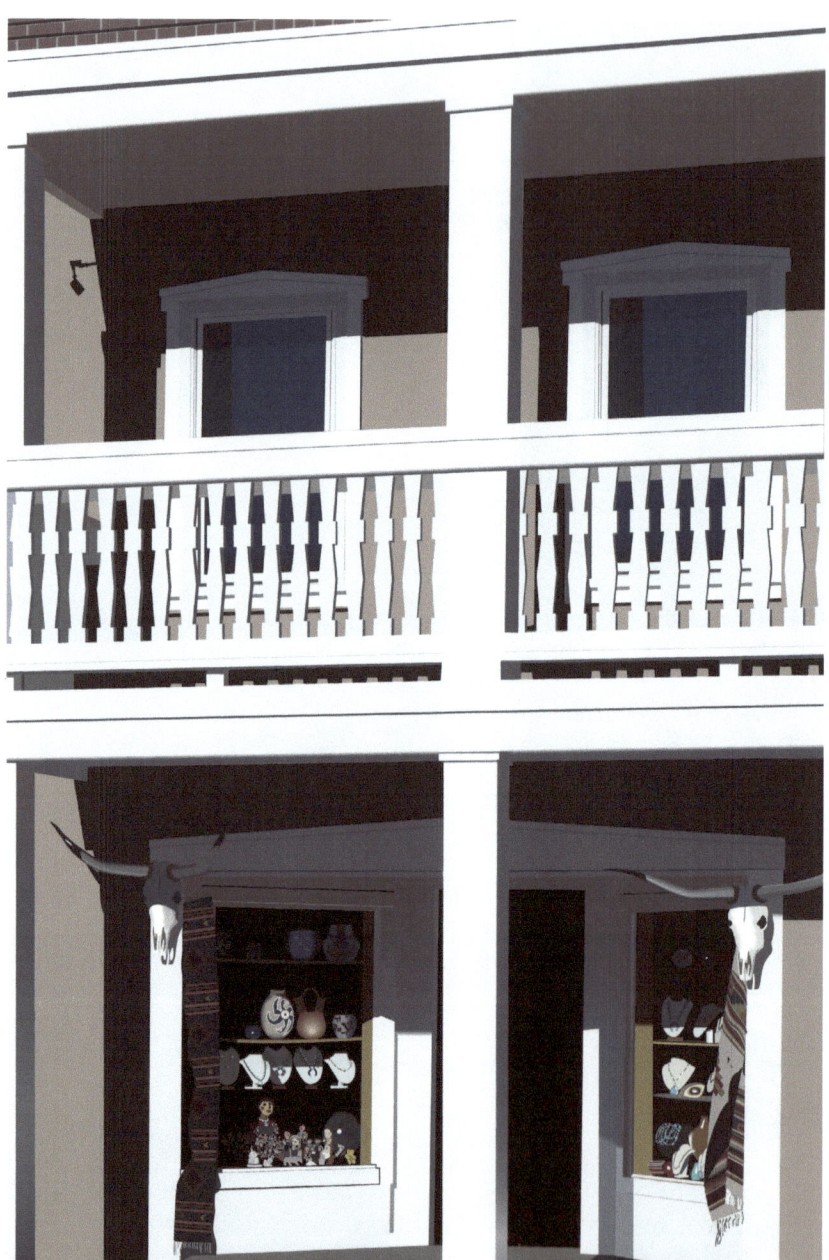

Shop 2 / Santa Fe

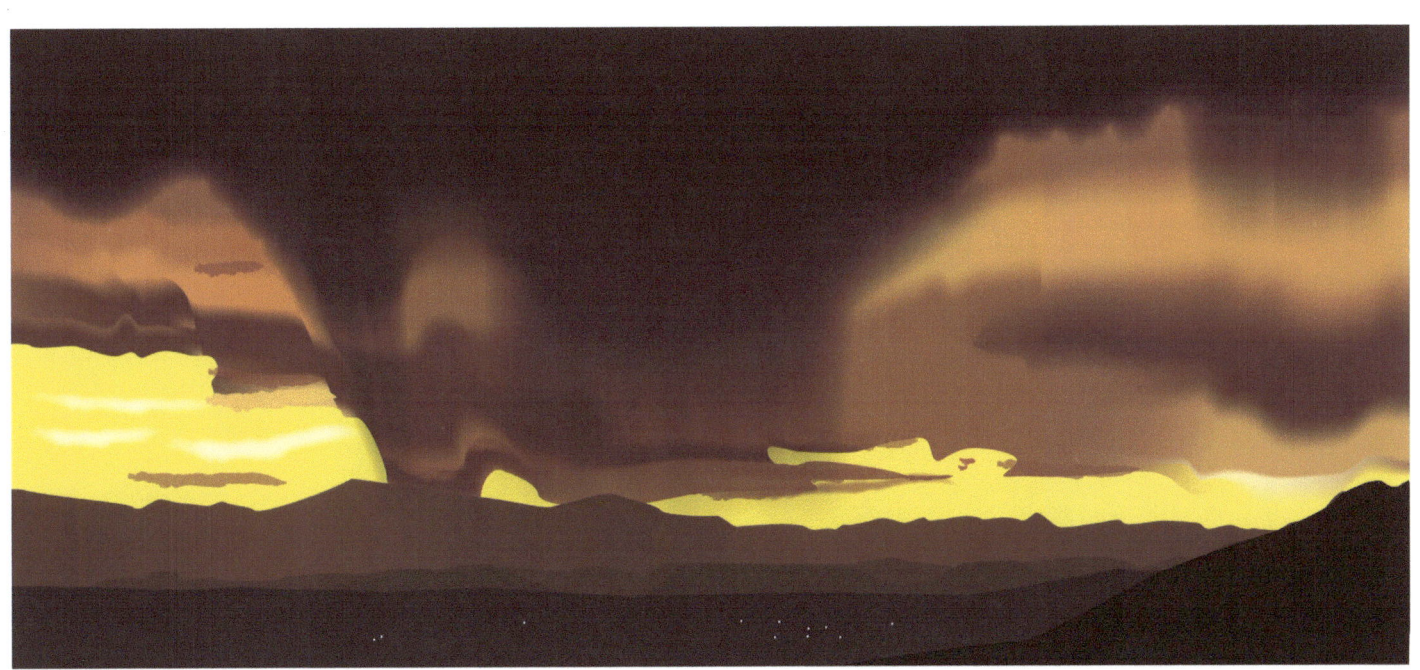

Monsoon Sunset / Santa Fe

Cliff Hauptman is a writer, photographer, and graphic artist. He is widely known for his many books and magazine articles about fishing. Original giclee prints of the drawings in this book may be purchased by emailing him at **cliff.hauptman@gmail.org.** Prices depend on size, which can be anywhere between 8"x 10" and 24"x 36" or larger.